INVESTING FOR TWENTY GOOD SUMMERS

INVESTING FOR TWENTY GOOD SUMMERS

Making your money work so you don't have to

MARTIN HAWES

ALLEN & UNWIN

First published in 2009

Allen & Unwin
83 Alexander Street
Crows Nest NSW 2065
Australia
Phone: (61 2) 8425 0100
Fax: (61 2) 9906 2218
Email: info@allenandunwin.com
Web: www.allenandunwin.com

National Library of Australia
Cataloguing-in-Publication entry:
Hawes, Martin, 1952–
Investing for twenty good summers : making your money work so you don't have to
ISBN 978 1 74175 689 0
1. Retirement—Planning. 2. Retirement income—Planning.
3. Finance, Personal.
332.024014

Set in 12/15.1 pt Adobe Caslon Pro
Designed and typeset by IslandBridge

Printed in Australia by McPherson's Printing Group

10 9 8 7 6 5 4 3 2 1

Contents

Introduction

Fifteen good summers

Now I am down to fifteen good summers.

When I wrote *Twenty Good Summers—work less, live more and make the most of your money*, I was 52 years old. Now I am 55: more summers have ticked by. They don't seem to go by any slower, in fact, quite the opposite. If twenty summers seemed a small, finite number, fifteen summers is getting positively scary!

I had the idea for *Twenty Good Summers* on my fiftieth birthday. I spent that day ice-climbing—climbing frozen waterfalls in the Remarkables range near my home in Queenstown. When I got to the summit that day, I did what I have done nearly every time I have reached the summit of a mountain in the area: I looked out at the sea of mountains which make up New Zealand's Southern Alps and contemplated all of the climbs that I must do 'one day'. However, as I was doing this, a thought occurred to me: I probably would not be doing this sort of climbing when I was 70—and today was my fiftieth birthday. Therefore I only had 20 good summers to do the climbs that I wanted.

This gave me a fright—twenty is a relatively small (and certainly finite) number. No longer does life stretch out ahead into the never-never. Whatever climbs I wanted to do, I had better get on and do them!

Since *Twenty Good Summers* was published, I have dealt with many clients who have wanted to rearrange their money so that they could work less and get on with living the lives that they want to live. To do this requires a whole new attitude and a whole new way of managing and investing money—both of which make up the theme and content of this book. It is a time for changes—unfortunately coming at a time of life when change no longer comes as easily as it once did. Nevertheless, if you want to change your life and have more time to do things, you are going to have to change your approach to money and investment. The key point is that you have to make the right changes—this is no time to make a major investment mistake.

Baby boomers are redefining 'retirement'. We are staring into the face of the end of full-time work and starting to think about how we will have to rearrange our money. We know that we will have to become reliant on investment returns for at least some of our income and some of us are not sure about how this will work. While I use the word often enough, I don't really like the idea of retirement. To me, the word 'retirement' has connotations of living a poor life, being hunched over a one-bar heater and reusing tea bags while you wait (usually in vain) for a visit from one of your children or grandchildren.

'Retirement' says to me that people have withdrawn from society; that they are no longer defined by what they do. One client said to me that before retirement she would tell people at social gatherings that she was an employment lawyer. People were interested in this and engaged in conversation. After she finished working, however, she would tell people that she was retired and she could see their eyes dart around the room looking for someone more interesting to talk to.

A better option for many is not to stop work but to slow down, to ease back into a comfortable semi-retirement where you still have some income from work and interest on investments, but also have more time to do the things that you have long promised yourself you would do 'one day'.

Virtually all of the clients I have seen in the last few years have not wanted to retire but instead to work less and ease back. As baby boomers we tend to see our latter years as a time when we can be actively engaged in our sports and hobbies, but also in work to some extent—possibly in voluntary work. Continuing in paid work is partly about earning additional income but partly about continuing to contribute to society. It can also be about giving our days some shape and structure. Many people now have a completely different idea of 'retirement' than their parents would have had.

Once you retire, you may want to work to some extent, but this work will probably not provide you with all of the income that you will need. Many people have to supplement the income that they receive from working less with income derived from their investment capital. This is, after all, exactly what the investment capital has been accumulated for: it is wealth you have built up for retirement and now is the time to start to use that wealth for the income that you need. This calls for a change to your investment strategy—you should no longer be aiming to build up wealth but instead your strategy should be about using your wealth to derive income.

Becoming reliant on income from investments is scary.

Anyone who can read a newspaper knows that investment returns are volatile, that they will not give the steady and regular income that is needed to fund living expenses. The losses that investors sometimes take are real—it is no fun to contemplate a diminished retirement fund when that is the only investment that you have.

If you are looking at investing for your retirement, you are likely to be a risk-averse investor. Much of this book is about reducing investment risk in its various forms. This book aims to give you some ideas to help you reduce the volatility of your investment portfolio and to structure your finances so that the returns that you receive are steady and smooth (or as steady and smooth as they can be). When you start to invest for twenty good summers, your aims will be different from when you were investing to build up a retirement nest egg. Because your aims are different, your investment strategy will also be different. This different strategy, aimed at steady and smooth income returns, is not talked about much in the media. The types of investments that you make and the way that you structure those investments is important. They will dictate whether you have good summers when you can ease your way into some kind of retirement or some tough summers where money is tight. Your investment approach has the potential to give you some years of great joy or of misery. There is little scope when investing later in life to make up for serious investment mistakes—this is something that you have to get right first time.

If there was ever a time to get on and do the things that you have always wanted to do, it is now. Whether it is having more time for family and friends, travelling, climbing frozen waterfalls or contributing to the community . . .

this is it. You will never be fitter and healthier than you are now—this is not a time to procrastinate. If you have built up some capital from years of work, now is the time to use that wealth to fund some good summers. Now is the time to rethink your investment strategy so that you stop growing your wealth and start using it for the purpose that you always intended—to live the life that you want.

Martin Hawes
June 2008

Chapter 1 | All change

Getting ready for some good summers

If you look at financial literature, you'll soon notice that nearly all of it is about building up wealth. Almost everything that is written about money assumes that you do not have enough money and that you need more. Financial seminars and courses are the same: they are aimed at making people rich (or at least better off). Almost all advice comes from the basic premise that you do not have enough money and that you need an investment growth strategy. However, this is not always true. There is a group who has quite different goals and risk profiles. This group—those who have fewer good summers left—needs a much less risky strategy and one that will give them income fairly reliably. This book is written for that group—baby boomers whose goal is no longer wealth accumulation but income from wealth.

From discussions with clients and questions I'm asked at conferences and seminars, I have learned two main things:

1. People really struggle with rearranging their money and investing differently. Most of us have had a lifetime of investing with the aim of building up wealth and starting to use capital to derive income requires a whole new approach.

2. Although most people are delighted when they are given a plan that will mean they don't have to go back into the office on Monday, there are some who are not so thrilled. These are people who really struggle to make the break, to change what they have done for decades. I do not think that this major change comes easily to anyone—just about everyone has some difficulties making it. And it is especially difficult later in life when no change comes easily. Some people find the idea of making the break to a new life so frightening that they don't make the change and carry on battling away in their work or business.

Sometimes these two difficulties are connected: some people struggle to make the break because they lack confidence that their investment capital can be used safely to give them the reliable income that they need. There is no doubt that money matters—and not simply a lack of money—stop people from making the move towards living the life of their dreams.

It is little wonder that a significant number of people do not feel that they can go boldly into a new life confident that they will have the income to fund it. People approaching retirement know that the way that they invest their money is important—they are at an age when they cannot afford any mistakes. They are wary of changing from earning their income through work (as they may have done for 40 years) to having it all come from investments. This is a major change.

People are right to be nervous of this change not only

because using capital to derive income is a new experience but also because a whole new financial strategy needs to be devised. Gearing (borrowing to buy investments) is a good idea for younger people looking to build wealth but is a seriously bad idea for older people wanting income. A strong emphasis on one asset class (for example, property or shares) may be acceptable for people in their thirties and forties, but is ridiculous for people in their sixties for whom diversification is essential. However, the habits of a lifetime are not easy to break, and I often struggle to convince clients that they should sell some of their properties or shares so that they can repay debt and have greater diversification. Again, the literature and seminars do not help: they are extolling the virtues of gearing or of owning several properties. They are, of course, right—gearing does work well. However, it is for wealth-building younger people and it is not for those of us who want to ease back and enjoy some summers.

Money and finance are about people and that's what keeps me engaged in the industry. The financial adviser's job is to find out what people's dreams and goals are and then to help them arrange their finances and investments to give them the life of their dreams. If we were all the same—if everyone had the same financial plan—I would have long since left the industry. I am still working as a financial adviser because I love to fit people with the right financial arrangements to help improve their lives. You need to acknowledge that you and your position are different from others and therefore recognise that some of the ideas and strategies that are laid out in books, article and seminars may not apply to you. To live well when you have started to ease back, you will have to unlearn much of what you learned about finance and investment to date, and put on blinkers and ear muffs so that you do not see and listen to information that is designed for other (usually much younger) people.

I know that making a break to a whole new life is scary. I know that the idea of living off the income from your investments is also scary. Perhaps you think that you do not have enough. Perhaps you know the volatility of the markets and wonder how you will cope when the investment returns do not appear in your account reliably every second Thursday. These worries (and others like them) can form a barrier that can stop you having the life that you want. Although these concerns can seem overwhelming when all rolled in together, when you isolate each one and then examine it carefully, none really has the ability to be a show-stopper. This is true of most worries that you might have in the financial area. I have found that people's worries about their finances are mostly a fear of the unknown, a fear that can be solved, rather than a dead end on the path to a better life.

Compromise for the life that you want

Most of the clients who I have seen over the last few years overestimate the amount of money that they need in order to start to ease back. Some have been people with millions of dollars of investment capital who have believed that they do not have enough to live on comfortably. Yet there have been others with much more modest amounts who have happily committed to a new life dependent on investment returns for income.

I believe that the difference in people's readiness to ease

back is mostly about how much they want to change and therefore how much and what they are prepared to compromise to get the things that are really important to them. Some people know the lives that they want—they have a very clear picture in their head of what it will be like when they are no longer working full-time—and are prepared to sacrifice some things to get the life of their dreams.

This is really about prioritisation and therefore about compromise. No one can have everything. We all have to decide what is important to us and trade some things off for others. This is much easier if you are very clear about what you *do* want—it is hard when you are not sure. The reason that I have been able to help people into retirement is because I usually spend a good bit of time clarifying exactly what it is that the client wants. When we know that, it becomes easier to make the compromises that are necessary.

In *Twenty Good Summers—Live more, work less and make the most of your money* I discussed how much money was enough. I said that the amount that I thought was needed to ease back was less than the amount that many financial advisers would say. The reason for that was that I identified seven variables which could be looked at and adjusted to make the numbers fit. These variables mean many people are able to reply to the question 'Do we have enough?' with the answer 'YES!'

People often put too much emphasis on money. Now, that might sound strange coming from someone like me, however I do think it important that you remain conscious of what the end game is. The end game is not a certain amount of money—it is the life that you want. Money is merely a tool to help you live the life that you want. It's a means to an end. Money is important and a certain amount of money will give you the life that you want. However, you may be able to achieve that life with a lesser amount of money. This can be really important if some kind of compromise or adjustment means that you can get on with the life of your dreams sooner than you might otherwise have thought possible.

To me, the most valuable thing that we have is time (followed closely by health). It seems crazy to me that you'd postpone having the life that you want if some relatively small compromise meant you could have it now. For example, you might be planning to ease back and semi-retire in five years time, and only do a four-month work contract each year. You have established the five-year time frame because you know that at that time you will have $250,000 invested and that this will give you $20,000 per annum income. Another way of doing this might be to do a bit more work—perhaps two three-month contracts instead of one four-month contract. This would let you ease back now rather than waiting for half a decade. It is relatively small compromises like this that can let you get on with the things that you are burning to do now rather than waiting (and running the risk that something derails your plans). The baby boomers have always been the 'now' generation—given the ever-diminishing number of summers that we have, I think it's better for you to get on with things now than wait.

However, first it's important for you to work out what it is you *do* want. Only if you are clear about that can you decide what you will give up to have it. Once you're clear on what you want, you need to consider the factors that allow you to answer the question 'do we have enough?' Of these factors there are five that deserve particular scrutiny. It is these five factors that are the areas where you can compromise. Each of these factors can be adjusted or played with so that you can make the numbers work and, in turn, change your life.

1. **Lifestyle**. Whatever your desired lifestyle, you will have to work out what it will cost. Do a budget for when you retire—the budget puts numbers around the lifestyle that you want or can afford. In doing that, you may be able to compromise on some spending if you cannot make the numbers work. For example, your desired lifestyle might include overseas travel twice a year. However, if you plan to only travel once a year (or even every second year) you may be able to ease back now. Is the travel really that important? If it is, you will probably have to keep working for a few more years so that you can grow your capital further, or look to compromise in some of the areas below.

2. **House**. Many people plan to downsize their houses to help them fund their retirement. However, when the time comes, this can be hard to do. It is not easy to give up that special location or the swimming pool that you put in a few years ago. Again, you have to decide what is important to you: do you want more time for family, golf and fishing now or do you want the swimming pool? Now is the time to think about what you *really* want.

3. **Inheritances**. Most of us want to leave some kind

of legacy—only a few people are genuinely happy to plan to go out on the last dollar and let the cheque for the undertaker bounce. However, the amount that you plan to leave your children will have a bearing on when you can start to ease back and the lifestyle that you will then have. Preparedness to spend capital (as opposed to simply spending income from capital) is a matter of degree—you can choose the amount that you are going to leave your family. For example, some people will plan to leave all of their wealth in inflation adjusted terms to the children; others might choose to spend all of their investment capital and then use a home equity release product to access some of the capital that they have in their house. Whatever you choose, this is another area where you may be prepared to compromise.

4. **Work.** This is a big one. The amount of work that you are happy to do when semi-retired is something that very easily lends itself to a compromise of sorts. For a few people, this is non-negotiable—they are not going to work at all. However, statistics show that more and more people are happy to do some work and for these people a compromise may be that they work an extra day, week or month a year so that they can start to enjoy some good summers sooner rather than later.

5. **Investment returns.** The investment returns that you expect to get can be adjusted to provide some compromise, however I would recommend caution.

> The risk and return equation is immutable: the greater the expected return, the greater the risk you will be taking. As will become clear later in this book, shares and property will give you the best returns and if you have a greater proportion of your portfolio in these areas you will, over long periods of time, have more income. However, these investments are also volatile—the returns will not be smooth and you could have months and years where you receive very little income. Therefore, you may invest a little more aggressively (i.e. have a little more in shares and property) but I do not think that you should take this too far.

Work out what your end game is—what do you really want? If you have a very clear picture of your dream life, you will know what you are heading towards and be able to make some of the hard compromises. More importantly, perhaps, if you know what it is that you really want, you will know what you will *not* compromise on. There are some things that you will not want to give away and there are others which will not make much difference to your overall happiness.

Remember that the important thing is not money. It is the quality of your life: your happiness, contentedness, satisfaction—call it what you will. That means working out the things that are important to you and letting money serve them. Money has no value in its own right but is only important for the quality of lifestyle that it can give you. More money usually means a better lifestyle but not always—some things do not require a lot of money. In any event, if you are prepared to compromise or go without some things, you may be able to have the things that are most important to you right now.

This book is not designed for wealth creators but for those with quite different goals. It is designed for those wanting income from their investments to fund their retirement. As such, it has a number of threads:

- It is likely that you will be dependent on your investment capital for at least some of your income. It is likely that you will continue to work to some extent (a very desirable thing for a number of reasons in my view). It is possible that you will have income from other areas (e.g. superannuation). Nevertheless, some of your income will come from the capital that you have built up over the decades. It is critical to the life that you want to lead that this income does not stop. You need to arrange your finances so that your investment returns are as smooth as possible and that you are never in a position where you can't buy the groceries.
- You are a risk-averse investor. Therefore you need to invest very safely and surely. Over the years, I have seen many people's lives destroyed by poor investment in retirement, their dreams shattered by a major investment loss. This book tries to make sure that this does not happen to you by recommending you adopt a 'safety first', highly diversified approach.
- You should go into retirement with no debts.

Gearing (or borrowing) for investment purposes may have helped to build up wealth. However, the first step to lowering risk is to get rid of any debts.

- One of the big risks that people in retirement face is inflation. Although inflation is nothing like as bad as it was in the 1970s and 1980s, there is always the risk that it will get away again and erode the spending power of your capital and income. This is underlined by the fact that you are likely to be dependent on income from your capital for a long time—life expectancy is improving and some people go into semi-retirement much earlier than previous generations did. My response to the risk of inflation is to make sure that you have some investments in property and shares, things that will give both income growth and capital growth and so help to keep up with inflation.

- Aversion to risk and the threat of inflation mean that asset allocation is very important. In fact, it is more than just 'very important', it is likely to be the make-or-break for your financial success. Asset allocation is simply how much of your capital you allocate to each of the different asset classes—that is, how much to shares or bonds and how much to put into emerging markets or property. Research shows that asset allocation makes the greatest difference between success and failure. Therefore you must—absolutely must!—get your asset allocation right from the start and then keep it right throughout your retirement.

- The investor's second biggest risk (after inflation) is becoming a forced seller. When there is a downturn in the markets, it is important that you do not have to sell to continue to put bread on the table. Markets always come back after a fall (although sometimes they can take a long time to do so). You have to arrange your money so that you are still in the market when they do come back. The way to do this is to hold some cash, perhaps enough to cover your living costs for one or two years while the markets are not performing. This cash acts as a buffer so that you do not have to sell investments at a bad time to fund your living expenses.
- Move slowly and gently into your new life and into your new financial arrangements. You should not sell out of markets all in one hit when you are going into retirement, and neither should you buy into markets all at one time. To make these big changes to your finances all on one day is to say that this is absolutely the right time to buy or sell, which may or may not be true, and if it is not true, you will face big losses. Instead, you should plan well in advance of retirement if you can, starting to sell down your existing portfolio well ahead of time. This will mean that you will not end up selling at a very poor time. The same is true for buying into your new investments—you should do it gradually rather than all on one day which may prove to be a very bad or a very good day.

Investment can be scary and becoming reliant on your investment returns does not come easily to many people. You have to purchase the groceries every week but the returns from investments are not always regular. Investment markets are volatile and it is no fun knowing that your investment capital has now been diminished due to events in New York or Zurich which are completely beyond your control. The ability to plan for a regular income from your investment capital that will match the regular expenses that you have is not easy. I hope this book will provide some ideas that will help you invest your money so that you can have the life that you want.

Chapter 2 | A whole new life, a whole new investment strategy

A change of lifestyle and circumstances necessitates a change to your investment strategy. The way that you have invested and managed your money to build up wealth will not serve you well when you come to use your capital to gain income. To a younger person who is investing to create wealth over a long period of time, volatility is little more than a nuisance, and may actually be helpful as down times in the markets can be used to buy cheap assets. However, for someone investing for income in retirement, down periods when investment returns are poor can change the prospect of 20 good summers into 20 bad summers. To such a person volatility is not just a nuisance—it can be downright destructive.

Investment is all about chance. As an investor you are continually working with the probability of the market changing—the returns that you will get and how often those returns disappoint. This is what risk is—it is the volatility of an investment type, the degree to which it goes up and down outside the performance that is expected, the amount that it deviates from the norm. Volatility risk is how often you should expect negative returns—a risky portfolio might be expected to see negative returns one year in four; a safe portfolio could perhaps see negative returns one year in ten.

Words like chance, probability and risk are used frequently (and synonymously) by professional investment advisors and investors. However this is not to say that investment is about luck or serendipity—there is much that you can do to increase the chance of your desired outcome. Furthermore, the simple recognition of the chance of particular things happening will improve the likelihood of you getting a good investment result.

There are many things that may happen within the investment world. There are many chances that an investor has to consider. For example:

- the chance that your bank will go into liquidation (a very slim chance)
- the chance that shares will give the best returns (a very high chance)
- the chance that your real estate investment trust (REIT) units will produce returns of 9 per cent (a very high chance)
- the chance that interest rates will fall (a 50/50 chance)

There is always uncertainty in investment in the short term, even though you can be fairly confident that something will or will not happen over the longer term. Statisticians and actuaries are the people who measure the probabilities of investment performance. They measure the returns that an investment is likely to achieve and the probability that it will underperform over certain periods of time. To do this, they look backward and study how investments have performed in the past. When they do this, they look back as far as they can—100 years or more if the information is available. While past performance is no guarantee of future performance, if the history of an investment class goes back long enough, the future ought to be much the same. Sure there may be some catastrophe that tips the world into something like the dark ages (in which case we don't have to plan for any good summers) but providing everything remains fairly normal, investment asset classes are likely to perform in the future pretty much as they have in the past.

Using the information derived from past performance, we are able to gauge future returns and the risk that in a certain time period those returns will not eventuate. For example, we can say that for a certain class of shares the returns will be 10.5 per cent and that you can expect one year of negative returns every four years; or that with some deposits you will get a return of 6 per cent and you could expect a year of negative returns every 50 years. You can take this further and look at a particular diversified portfolio and say that this will return 8 per cent and there will be negative returns every 12 years.

Time

Note that time is a very important factor in investing—we are constantly talking about the chance of something happening within a certain time frame. We know that certain things are going to happen but we do not know when. We can only therefore say that there is a chance of something happening within a certain time period, and calculate the likelihood within that time period. The longer the time period, the greater the chance of something, either good or bad, happening. For example, the chance of there being a major 1930s style depression with many bank failures before the end of next week is very low. However, the chance of something like that happening within the next 100 years is quite high. Similarly, the chance of shares giving a return at the rate of 10 per cent per annum this calendar year is fairly low, but the chance of them producing this over the next 50 years is quite high.

Unfortunately, those investing in retirement for income do not have the amount of time that a younger person has to increase the chance of the good things happening. Younger people can afford to ignore volatility because if their investments go down, they have time for them to revert to the norm and go back up again. They know that over long periods of time they will get the expected returns even though they may have to endure a roller coaster ride while getting them.

Older investors, however, lack time and also need to adopt a strategy so that the down times are shorter and shallower. They need to know that their money will be there when they need it. It is this time frame that is so important—the last thing that you want is to have to sell investments in a downturn.

The easiest way to reduce volatility to almost zero is to have all investment capital as cash in a few banks. If you do this you are likely to have very low volatility, however you will also have very low returns. Even as a very conservative investor, you need to allocate some of your capital to more volatile assets (shares and property) to give you better returns and to take care of inflation. You should note that having all of your money in banks does not reduce your volatility to absolutely zero. If you do this for long enough, one or more of your banks will fail and so you will suffer a loss. There is no such thing as an absolutely risk-free investment.

Your overall strategy should be to get solid returns with the lowest possible volatility. To achieve adequate returns, you simply must have some growth assets (shares and property) even though they are more volatile. The alternative is to invest in fourth-rate finance companies and this is likely to be more risky than owning good quality shares and property! To have good returns with moderate volatility means allocating your capital to assets across the investment classes to give you good diversification.

You could, if you have enough money, solely invest in bank deposits but this would give you no income growth and expose you to the vagaries of inflation or even a return to hyper-inflation. This is another chance (or risk) that you have to manage and you manage it by owning some shares and some property. Owning these growth assets will mean some volatility—that is, a chance of some years with losses. To a degree, you have to choose between one risk and another by asking yourself what is the greater risk, inflation or occasional years when you have investment losses.

Expectations

We all know that there will be negative returns at times—that should never come as a surprise. Given that you are unlikely to be wealthy enough to simply put all of your capital in several banks or in government bonds, that you could not cope with the insidious effects of inflation and that you need to get higher returns, you must expect to experience some volatility. This may sound like an obvious thing to say, however every time there is a large fall in markets, people behave as if they weren't aware of the possibility that they might get negative returns. I find this level of surprise really quite extraordinary. Financial planners and investment advisers the world over tell of the work that they have to do allaying clients' fears when markets turn bad. There is a lemming-like rush to the exit door—a rush that is almost always too late. The shock of negative returns results in losses because investors often sell out at this time of market weakness.

You should expect poor returns at times and those poor returns will sometimes be negative. There is nothing that you can do about these gloomy bad times except know that they will happen and arrange your investments with that expectation. This expectation and planning will mean:

- that you are well diversified across all asset classes
- that you continually rebalance your portfolio so that your asset allocation and diversification remain as they are meant to be
- that you maintain a reservoir of cash to live on while returns are bad.

All of these things are dealt with in subsequent chapters. Suffice to say at the moment that it is crazy not to expect tough times in investment markets and even crazier not to plan for them.

Asset allocation

Asset allocation is so important that it has its own chapter (chapter 5). Asset allocation is the proportion of your capital that you assign to each asset class: how much to shares, how much to property, how much to bonds and how much to bank deposits. Note that when you consider these asset classes, we need to recognise that there are different ways to get exposure to each. For example, you may want to put 20 per cent of your portfolio into property. You could do this by directly buying a property (perhaps more than one property if the allocation is great enough). Alternatively, you could buy into a real estate investment trust (REIT) (see page 154). Although there are pros and cons of investing directly by buying a property and investing indirectly through REITs, both give you the desired exposure to the property asset class.

It is asset allocation more than anything else that will dictate your returns and the amount of volatility risk. Provided that you have not been stupid and have only a limited number of investments in each asset class—for example, only one bond for your allocation to bonds or only two or three shares each in the same industry and in the same country—it will be the proportion that you have in each asset class that will make the difference. It is asset allocation that will mean that you can either start to plan some good climbing trips or start to look at the situations vacant section of your local newspaper.

It is this part of your investment strategy that you should plan more than any other. It should not only be planned at the start but you also need an easy means of monitoring it so that you are sure that it stays fairly close to the percentages that you set. This is called 'rebalancing' and is necessary because each of the asset classes will change in value differently over time, meaning that the allocation that you had at the beginning will soon change.

For example, on retirement you may set your asset allocation like this:

Shares	25%
Property	15%
Bonds	30%
Cash deposits	30%

However, imagine that there is a boom in bonds but a fall in share values. This could result in you changing your portfolio to look like this:

Shares	15%
Property	15%
Bonds	40%
Cash deposits	30%

To rebalance, you would need to sell 10 per cent of your bonds and purchase 10 per cent of shares to bring your portfolio back to where it should have been. This may be hard to do because the profits that you have from your bonds will encourage you to hold onto them and the fall in share prices will mean that you are very reluctant to go against the tide and buy more. Nevertheless, that is what you should do. The discipline imposed by rebalancing and selling some of your bonds will mean that you are taking some of your profits. You will be selling into a strong market, which is just what you should be doing. On the other side, the additional shares that you buy will be bought at a time of weakness. This can seem like a hard thing to do because of the negative noise that is coming out of the markets, but it is the right thing to do.

This does not have to be done precisely. In fact, it cannot be done exactly because the proportions in your portfolio will change constantly. For myself, I rebalance if any one of my asset classes gets more than 10 per cent out of line with the allocations that I have set. You do not need to constantly look at your asset allocation but it is something that you should watch fairly regularly, especially when there are major movements in the various markets. Those who are not managing their investments directly but who have employed a financial adviser to look after their money, should be very careful to ask the financial adviser about rebalancing. There are some I have known who look at rebalancing once a year. This is not frequent enough—you need someone who will monitor your investments more closely than this. For many people this rebalancing should be done on a monthly basis. Having nothing more than an annual review is completely inadequate.

Diversification

Asset allocation and diversification go together. How you allocate your investment capital between the asset classes and among investments within those classes determines your diversification. Some young people may have very little diversification because they have all of their wealth in just one asset class, often property. By having everything in that one asset class, they have very little diversification—which may be reasonable for them because they are prepared to take a risk with property and are backing themselves to manage it well and produce good profits. They have income from their jobs and so can withstand the periodic downturns that property values experience. Those of us investing for income in our latter years, however, do not have a great deal of other income so we must diversify to minimise the investment slumps that happen every few years.

Diversification is not solely about spreading your investment capital around so that you do not have all your eggs in one basket, it can get quite a lot more sophisticated than that. One important aspect is that you should try to choose investments that do not show returns which are correlated to each other.

There are some investments which have a tendency to go up in value at the same time as another investment is going down. Economic and investment theory says that the time in the economic cycle when interest rates rise means that economic times are very good. The good economic times are very good for share values (they are going up) but the increase in interest rates is very bad for bonds (they go down in value—see chapter 10). Therefore, the returns from bonds and shares are not positively correlated—one tends to go up while the other is going down. If you have some bonds and some shares in your portfolio, the bad times from one will tend to be cancelled out by the good times from the other. Owning more than one asset class tends to hedge the falls in the other classes.

Things do not work out perfectly like this all of the time, of course. There are times when all asset classes rise or fall together. However, one investment or group of investments hedging another does happen frequently enough and this is something that you should think about.

Capital gain versus income

In the olden days, people used to pick up their gold watch and retire at the age of 60. They had a life expectancy of about ten more years and so they cashed in their superannuation and put their money in the bank (and perhaps bought into a bit of government stock). Shares and property were largely ignored. Now retirement, or some form of it, is for a much longer period—you might start to ease back at the age of 60 and may live well into your eighties—and you are investing for a generation. With this likely period of time, some growth investments are going to be necessary to provide additional returns and to cover inflation.

There are some growth investments that pay out very little by way of cash returns. Even though a company may be quite profitable and/or have very good prospects, it can pay out either no dividends or only very small ones. A good example of this at the moment would be Google. Most income investors would ignore Google shares as an investment as the shares do not pay dividends. However, assuming you think that Google is a good company and its shares are likely to grow in value, as an income investor you could buy Google shares even though they do not pay dividends.

What would you do for income? My answer to that is that you would sell some Google shares when necessary and take out your capital profits. If you have been proven right and the shares have indeed gone up in value, you might sell a percentage of shares equivalent to the percentage that they have risen in the past year or so.

Selling up to access capital profits can have tax advantages. Many countries have either no capital gains tax or capital gains taxes that are fairly benign and less costly than income taxes. Therefore, all else being equal, a capital profit that you can take by selling a few units or shares is better than an income-producing investment. This opens up a whole range of investments to income investors—investments which were previously thought to be unsuitable for older investors.

Liquidity

People pay too much for liquidity. By this I mean that there are some investments that are offered at low yields because they are able to be liquidated easily. For example, an issuer may sell a bond promising that there will be a market for the sale of the bond should you need to cash up. Such a bond would likely be offered at a higher price (which would mean a lower yield) than the same bond if there was no way that it could be liquidated before maturity.

People like the idea of liquidity. They want the option to be able to cash up and the flexibility that this affords. Therefore they are happy to pay extra for the more liquid investment but, in my view, they pay too much. Most people investing for their retirement are investing for quite long periods. This may change as you get older but I can see no difficulty with a 65 year old buying into an illiquid six-year bond. Why would they want to cash this up? Surely such a person would be better to have the additional yield than to give up some return so that they have the flexibility to cash up.

Clearly you need to be very careful to make sure that the investment is a good one and that you are not going to need to cash up before maturity. You should, in any event, have a range of different maturity dates with the bonds that you own. Your investment structure should mean that you have bonds and other investments maturing fairly regularly (see chapter 9). On the whole, investors should not pay much, if anything, for liquidity. It is not a lot of use if you can arrange things so that you do not need it.

Timing

I am sorry to say that I have seen many people have their lives wrecked because of poor timing. These have not been people who have gone out and deliberately tried to time the market. Instead, they are people who have cashed up by selling their business, farm, property portfolio or superannuation funds. Being cashed up, they have looked around to invest for income, usually taking advice from a financial adviser. When they have received their advice and agreed that the set of investments that have been recommended are suitable, they have them handed over their lump sum and gone ahead and executed the investment plan all on one day. This day may prove to be a very good time to invest but may also prove to be a very bad time. For many people it turns out to be a bad time and their investment capital is destroyed and their plans for good summers are shattered.

In recent years we have had great booms, with very high values in many markets, making it a very bad time to invest.

When the markets turn down the investor is left high and dry with large losses. A much better time to invest is when things are gloomy and markets are tough. However, few people do invest in these times because the media is full of doom and gloom.

It is not a good idea to invest all of your investment capital at once. Dollar cost averaging (a flash term for drip feeding your money into markets over a period of time) is essential if you are to manage timing risk. This is covered in Chapter 9.

In summary, you will need to think about a new way of investing:

- Diversify—have as many different investments as possible.
- Have some money offshore—money in another country is the ultimate form of diversification.
- Have some growth assets (shares and property)—you need these to keep up with and cover the risk of inflation.
- Own some non-income producing investments—being prepared to occasionally sell some units means that you do not have to forgo some very good investment opportunities.
- Expect some bad investment years—knowing that bad stuff will happen means that you will be ready for it.
- Hold a good amount of cash—this is the buffer that

will smooth out your returns so that you can always buy the groceries.

- Decide the degree to which you are going to manage your investments yourself—there are pros and cons for this but only you can decide.
- When you have decided what asset classes you are going to invest in, look for the best way to get exposure to these investment areas—there can be lots of ways to profit from different markets.
- Invest any lump sum slowly—you should probably take several years to become fully invested.

An investment strategy will always be something of a moving target. It is not something which is set in stone, never changing. As markets change, your strategy will change. Your strategy will also change as your circumstances change. If you are reading this as a 66 year old, you have to recognise that your situation is likely to be different when you are an 82 year old. Your investment strategy will need to change with your circumstances. Moreover, your investment portfolio and the way that you manage your money will probably never turn out exactly as you plan. You should think of your plan as the template that you are constantly moving towards rather than something that is to be achieved and ticked off a list. The markets are constantly changing and your investment approach has to change with the times. It is the constant change in people's lives along with constant change in what is going on in the world which, to me, makes investment so fascinating.

Chapter 3 | Only four investments

Investment seems confusing to many people because there are so many options. You open the newspaper and there are pages of investments with their prices: shares, managed funds, bonds, gilts, hedge funds, finance companies, REITs, unit trusts, insurance bonds. There are columns of these things, all from different providers and with advertisements for them nearby making competing claims for your money. If you are confused to the point of simply putting all your money in the bank and forgetting it, you are forgiven.

You can start to divide and categorise investments in all sorts of ways. In my book *Twenty Good Summers,* I distinguished between 'ownership assets' and 'debt assets'. The first of these, ownership assets, are things where you are the owner of enterprise as with shares and property; the second, debt assets, are when you are lending your money to the enterprise as with bank deposits or bonds. Diagrammatically, it looks like this:

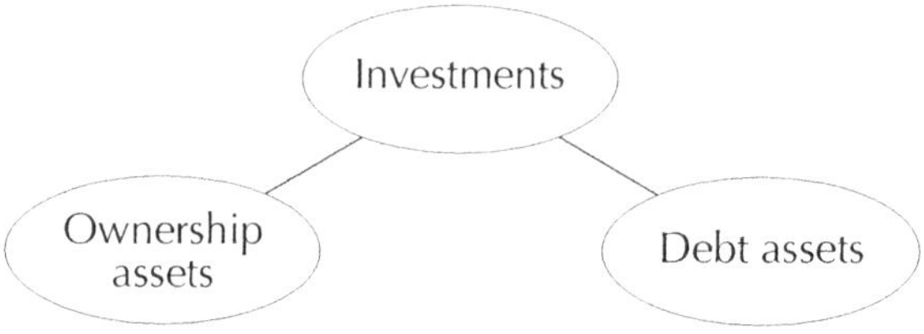

These two categories can be split further. Ownership assets can be split into shares and property. Debt assets are largely split by the length of time that you are making the investment for. That is between short-term deposits, which are often with a bank, and longer-term ones, which are usually known as bonds although they can also be known as stocks. The division between the two of these is a bit arbitrary. You can have a one-year bond or a one-year term deposit with a bank and we could argue about which category these should go in. Nevertheless, from an investment point of view, there is certainly a difference between a long-term deposit and a short-term one, even though we may argue where the dividing line is. Diagrammatically, this split looks like this:

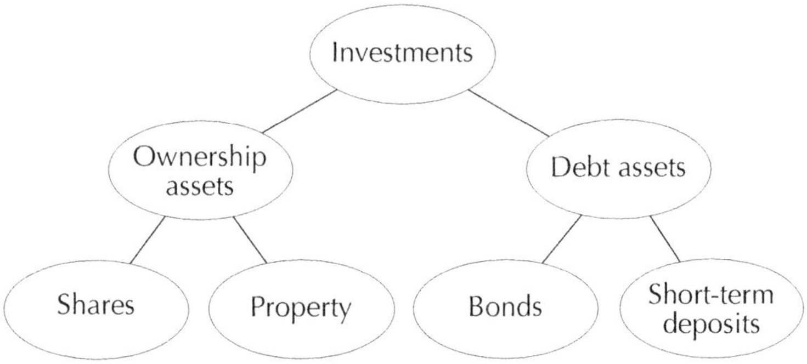

Clearly, each of these categories could be split further. Property can be split into industrial, commercial and residential property. Bonds can be split between corporate bonds and government stock. Shares can be split almost to infinity by industry or country. However, everything that is really an investment should fit into one of these four categories and when we are considering asset allocation issues, I think that it is useful to stop at these four categories.

Assets to allocate

The four main asset classes are:

Shares

Property

Cash/deposits

Bonds

These are the four asset classes that you will have to allocate your capital to. The proportion of your capital that you will allocate to each will make the greatest difference to the returns that you receive and the volatility that you experience. You will want to have some money invested in each one of these asset classes but not in equal measure. The way that you mix and match them is one of the biggest investment decisions that you make and is discussed in chapter 5. This chapter makes it very clear that you must get your allocation to each of these asset categories right—everything else is much less important. Too much in one category will mean that you either have very poor returns but low volatility or very good returns but very high volatility. For example, if you have nearly everything in bank deposits, you will sleep very easily at night because you will only very rarely have an investment loss (you might have to wait 50 years before you had a loss). However, your returns will be very low. On the other hand, if you have nearly everything in shares, you will certainly get good returns over a long period of time. However, you would need to invest a great deal in sleeping pills because you will have a lot of nights sitting up worrying.

Shares

Shares are often also known as equities and are simply a share in a business (in the USA shares are often called stock while in many other countries, stock means bonds—more confusion!). By investing in shares, you are buying a part of a business and its assets and will therefore get a part of its profits. There are all sorts of businesses in many different industries and countries and, when buying shares, you can and should diversify by investing in many of these.

Property

Property (also known as real estate) for investment purposes covers buildings and land that have an income return in the form of rent. This means that the property asset class includes residential as well as commercial property and, more rarely, farms. In my view the property asset class does not include sites and sections as these do not provide income.

Cash/deposits

This asset class is mostly about bank deposits but can include things like cash management trusts and other short-term deposits. This is a very important asset class for older investors, as you will see in chapter 10.

Bonds

These are long-term debt investments. You lend your money to a corporation or a government for a fixed term and get an agreed amount of interest throughout the life of the investment. The term of the investment (known as the maturity) is usually several years but can range as long as 30 years. Many bonds can be bought and sold on a secondary market after they have been taken out. Bonds are also known as fixed interest or occasionally as stock.

Other 'investments'

The thing that these four asset classes have in common is that they provide income. Property has income from rents, shares have income from the profits that the business makes and cash/deposits and bonds have income in the form of interest.

However, many people ask me about other things that are often called 'investments'—things like gold, jewellery, antiques, art and suchlike. What sort of investments are these? The answer is that they are not investments at all. My definition of an investment is that it must have income as shares, property, cash/deposits and bonds have. When you are investing, you are buying an asset for the income that is derived from it—you are effectively handing over your money and getting an income stream in return. Sometimes this income stream will be great, at other times it will be relatively small.

Some investments provide an income stream that is secure and certain; others have an income stream which is uncertain and risky. Sometimes the income stream will grow, other times it will stay static or even decline. Nevertheless, whatever the quantity or the quality of the income, investments provide income—that is what defines them.

Other things that people sometimes call investments, for example gold, art or antiques, have no income and are therefore not truly investments. When you buy these things, the only way that you can make money from them is by selling them for more than you paid for them. You may be able to do that, if you have some expertise in art or antiques. However, you need to recognise what it is that you are doing. You are buying something in the expectation or hope that someone else will pay more for it. This is speculating rather than investing.

There is a world of difference between speculation and investment. On the one hand the article that you are speculating on has value only because of its beauty or rarity. There is usually a market for these things but that market is based on things other than income. Investments (shares, property, cash/deposits and bonds) have a worth and a value that is based on their income. Another investor will buy the bond that you own based on how much income it has, the security of that income and for how long the income will continue. As shown later in this chapter, all investments are valued by both the quantity and the quality of the income that they provide. If you are to understand investment, it is critical that you understand how this works. The principles are the same for each asset class, although the vocabulary differs. Buying an investment for an income stream is obviously quite a different prospect from buying art, antiques or gold.

I am not saying that you should not speculate in art, jewellery, gold or the like but I would say that you should do so with a very small amount of money. It may be that you know about these things and can do quite well out of them. The important thing to understand is that these things are not investments and should not be thought of as such. Investments must have income—it is income that makes something an investment. If you are offered something which has no income or no prospect of income recognise it for what it is—something to speculate or bet on rather than something to invest in.

Managed funds

There are other things that people frequently call investments but are not in the four asset classes set out above. These are managed funds, things like unit trusts, superannuation funds, property syndicates and REITs. These are not investments in their own right but are instead a means to investment. Managed funds work by pooling investors' money, and appointing a manager who then invests in one or more of the four asset classes. Thus we get managed funds that are based on property, shares, or bonds and deposits (or sometimes a combination of all of them).

Although not strictly an investment, they are a means or vehicle to one of the four asset classes and so should be considered as investments. Managed funds effectively give you exposure to the asset class or market of your choice. For example, if you want to invest in shares but know nothing about shares, you do not want to do it yourself. You should therefore find a good share manager who offers a managed fund based on shares. Invest in that fund and you should get an investment performance that is very close to what the sharemarket returns—it will be better or worse than average sharemarket return depending on how good the manager is. Managed funds can give you exposure to just about any asset class or market that you want, from eastern European property to emerging markets' shares.

This is why when I talk of having 20 per cent of your portfolio in shares that I don't necessarily mean that you will directly own the shares yourself. Instead, I mean that you will have 20 per cent of your portfolio exposed to the performance of the sharemarket. This exposure may be because you have bought the shares directly yourself or it may be that all of your shares are via managed funds or it could be, as it is in my own case, a combination of directly held shares and managed funds. Whether you invest directly yourself or by means of managed funds is a major decision that you will have to take, one that is covered in chapter 11. However, whichever way that you go, it is the amount that you allocate to each of the four asset classes that will make the biggest difference to your performance, and not the means that you choose to invest through.

Investments have income and are valued by that income

As already outlined, all investments are valued by the income streams that they have. This is based on the quantity of the income and also on the quality of the income. Income quality is judged by factors such as whether the income appears to be sustainable, how secure it is and whether it is growing. For example, if a bond is paying interest of $1000 pa, it will be valued significantly higher if it was issued by a government rather than a corporate. This is because the government would be considered to have much better ability to meet the interest payments in good times and bad because governments have the right to tax and seldom renege on their obligations. The fact that the government bond would cost more than the corporate bond would be reflected in the yield that you would get as an investor. Because you have paid more for the $1000 pa income stream, the yield or interest rate from the government bond would be lower than the corporate one.

This principle stands for all investments. Investors will pay more or less for a certain amount of income according to the income's quality. Although the general principle is that all investments are valued by the amount and quality of the income that is likely to come from them, this is expressed differently for each of the asset classes as each asset class has its own language and vocabulary. Below is a brief outline of how each asset class is valued. If you are to be an active investor, I would encourage you to research further into valuation of investment assets.

Shares

Shares are valued by their net, after-tax earnings or profits. It is likely that only a part of that profit is paid out to shareholders by way of dividends. A good proportion of a company's earnings are retained by the company to fund ongoing activities and growth. Even though earnings are retained by the company, they add to the company's value and one day will go to shareholders. Therefore, to value a company's shares we look at total after tax earnings, ignoring the fact that some of those earnings are not paid out to shareholders.

To value a company, we need to first work out how much of the company's profit is attributable to one share. This is called **earnings per shares (eps).** Earnings per share are calculated by dividing the earnings of a company by the number of shares on issue.

$$\textbf{eps} = \frac{\textbf{annual earnings}}{\textbf{shares on issue}}$$

If we take a company that is earning \$40 million and has 100 million shares on issue, its earning per share is calculated like this:

$$\textbf{eps} = \frac{\textbf{\$40m}}{\textbf{100m}} = \textbf{40 cents}$$

This means that 40 cents of the company's earnings are attributable to each share.

Now we need to look at what we are prepared to pay for that 40 cents, that is how much is each share to be valued at given that each year it is going to earn 40 cents. We do this by looking at something called a **price:earnings ratio (P:E).** A P:E ratio compares the price (or value) of each share to the earnings of each share. It is the number of years that the earnings per share would need to be made to equate to the price.

$$\text{P:E} = \frac{\textbf{price of each share}}{\textbf{earnings per share}}$$

Put another way, we can decide what the value of a share should be if we can judge what an appropriate P:E ratio is for that particular company. This judgment is made by knowing the market and looking at what P:E ratios other similar companies sell for. For example, if we judged that the P:E for the above company which is earning 40 cents per share should be 12, we could say that its value should be 480 cents (i.e. its reasonable value would be 12 times its earnings). If the company was trading at less than 480c, its shares would rate as buy; if more than 480c, a sell. The P:E ratio tells you what fair value should be.

This is a very simple explanation of valuing shares. The important thing is that investors look at how many times the income from the company's share would need to be gathered to pay for that share. If it's a small number of times, the company share is cheap; if it is a high number of times, it is expensive. As an investor, you should continually assess what you are prepared to pay for a particular income stream.

Property

Property investors look at the income that they will get from a property by way of rent and then judge what sort of yield they should be receiving. The rental figure is easily established and known and when a judgment is made on what a reasonable yield should be, the value can be struck. The only way to get the yield that you want is to adjust the rental price. Note that the rent that is used in making this calculation is the net rental, that is the rent after costs like rates, insurance and maintenance have been deducted.

The rental yield is very easy to calculate:

$$\text{Yield} = \frac{\textbf{net rental}}{\textbf{property value}} \times 100$$

If a property has a net annual rental of $25,000 pa and the asking price for the property is $450,000, at that value the yield would be:

$$\text{Yield} = \frac{\$25,000}{\$450,000} \times 100 = 5.6\%$$

As a prospective purchaser of this property you now have to decide whether a yield of 5.6 per cent per annum is enough for you buy the property. If it is not enough, the only way that you can get a higher yield is to pay less for the property. The lower the yield that you are prepared to accept, the more expensive the property is.

Cash/deposits

Cash and other short-term deposits are only different from bonds insofar as the maturity is longer. The valuation of these, on the rare occasion that valuation is needed, is the same as for bonds.

Bonds

Bonds are offered and sold with a fixed amount of interest for a certain length of time. In some ways they are riskier than cash and short-term deposits because the interest is fixed over the full term of the investment. For example, if you purchased a ten-year bond and inflation and interest rates rise over the period of the bond, you may end up receiving interest rates that are well below the current market. The ten-year bond may have been sold to you yielding 6 per cent interest but that may not seem such a good deal three years later when prevailing interest rates are 8 per cent. You, of course, are stuck with this relatively low interest rate unless you can sell the bond to someone else.

You may well be able to sell the bond to someone else because there is a secondary market for many bonds. The trouble is, if interest rates have risen to 8 per cent, no one is going to give you the amount that you had paid for the bond because then they would only get 6 per cent interest and they could buy similar bonds at 8 per cent. The buyer will, therefore offer you a price that is less than what you had paid for it, a price that would see the buyer getting the equivalent of the prevailing market rate—i.e. 8 per cent. This happens frequently and people often do take losses on bonds.

More positively, the converse also happens. Investors do make capital profits from bonds when interest rates fall. The same investor who bought the bond at 6 per cent could find that interest rates fall and the prevailing rate drops to 4 per cent. The investor could simply hold the bond through to maturity, enjoying the additional interest that is being paid. Alternatively, the investor could instruct his or her broker to sell the bond to receive more than what was originally paid. Many investors do trade bonds in this way, trying to pick future interest rates to make a profit.

There are four main things that dictate the value of a bond:

- The prevailing interest rate in the market at the time
- The credit-worthiness of the issuer. Clearly a bond issued by the US government would be much more attractive and expensive than one issued by a small company in Fiji.
- The duration or maturity of the bond—i.e. when your capital will be repaid. A bond that does not mature for ten years will usually be less expensive

than one which matures in three years. All else being equal, most investors do not want to lock up their money for very long periods of time.

- The liquidity of the bond—i.e. whether or not there is an active secondary market allowing investors to cash up if necessary. Generally, a bond that has a strong secondary market will be more expensive than one where you are locked in. Note my previous comments that investors often pay too much for liquidity.

This is a very brief overview of how shares are valued. Professional and institutional investors have often spent years at university learning the principles of investment valuation, and then more years of practical experience in the markets learning to judge what they should pay for an earnings stream in any particular market at any particular time. To be an active investor there is much more to learn. The key thing to remember is that for an asset to be classed as an investment it must have income. It will then be valued by that income and how the income changes over time.

Chapter

4 | Investment risk

There is no such thing as risk-free investment. There is nothing that you can do with your money that does not carry some risk of a loss. Even the safest of investments can fail: banks have gone broke in the past and even governments have reneged on their obligations at times. Right from the start you need to acknowledge risk and expect there to be losses at times. The acknowledgement of risk and expectation of possible losses is important. Knowing that all investment carries risk will mean that you will do what you can to avoid big losses.

People investing for income so that they can enjoy twenty good summers are the most risk-averse group of investors that I know. Sometimes they don't behave in a risk-averse way though. I have often enough seen older investors use gearing (borrowing) to enter into very risky investments with a good slug of their capital. I think that people often go on investing in the way that they have always invested without altering their investment strategy when their lifestyle has changed. Habits are hard to break but you need to recognise that as you stop, or slow down, working, your risk profile changes. You are no longer trying to build up wealth; you are now looking for income. No longer do you have income from full-time work; income which can paper over investment mistakes or market volatility.

However, there is something else even more important than not having income. As you get older, you no longer have as much time. This is important in two respects:

1. If you make a major mistake and have a very big loss, perhaps because you are not well diversified, you have neither the income from work nor the time to restore your finances. As a result, you will have little income on which to live.

2. Even when you are well diversified, a market may move against you. While the market will, in time, move back up, the down period can be very difficult in the meantime. This risk of market volatility is discussed further in this chapter.

There is a great deal that you can do to manage investment risk. Recognising that there are risks involved with any investment strategy is a good start because it means that you can actually do something about it. At the start of their retirement many people adopt a strategy that is excessively risk averse in some ways. That is, they invest in a way that seems too low risk. In acknowledging risk, you should also recognise that you must take *some* risk.

Twenty or thirty years ago the vast majority of people retired at age 60. On the day of their retirement, they picked up their superannuation savings or cashed in their investments and went off to their retirement party where they were given a gold watch or a rocking chair. On the day after their retirement party, they set out to invest their capital.

The standard advice they would receive was that they need to invest wholly in 'income assets' such as bank deposits, bonds and company debentures. Shares and property were regarded as too risky.

This strategy might seem low risk. However, it is not. First, all of the retiree's money is in just one asset class. While this asset class is the lowest risk one, it could still be badly affected by certain economic times. Having all of your capital in one asset class, even the least risky one, is not a good idea.

Second, because they are looking for income, people can be tempted into higher risk company bonds or debenture stock. These third or fourth tier companies may offer higher interest rates but they only do so because they have to, as the market knows that they are dodgy and they can only raise money by offering high returns.

Third, on retirement you have the risk of inflation. The thing about income assets is that they have no growth—neither income growth nor capital growth. You may be dependent on the income from your investment capital for a very long time and you therefore need the growth that comes from shares and property. In a way there is a 'risk' that you might live for a long time!

Volatility risk

Most people see investment risk in terms of the possibility of their investments collapsing. The basic fear is that one or more of the things that you put your money into will turn out to be duds and that you will take a loss. If the investment crashes and burns, the loss is permanent, resulting in an impaired lifestyle. In fact, if you are well diversified, this is almost certain to happen to one or two of your investments at times. You should expect it because if you have a whole range of different investments there are bound to be significant losses on some of them. Someone who is well diversified will still not actively *enjoy* an investment loss but it will at least not affect overall lifestyle.

The other way of looking at risk is in terms of volatility. This is the way that most professional investment advisers and fund managers think of risk. In fact, when investment risk is being measured, it is volatility that is having the ruler run over it.

Volatility is the amount of thrashing around that an investment does as it achieves its expected returns. It is measured by something called standard deviation. An investment is expected to produce a certain return and standard deviation measures how often the investment will vary from this expected return. A good way of looking at this is to think of shares. These are a very volatile form of investment so we might expect an investment in a basket of shares to have negative returns every four years. Bonds are a much less volatile investment and so negative returns may only be experienced every seven years.

The question for you as an investor is: how often can you tolerate negative returns? Most of us who are reliant on our capital for income will answer this by saying 'not very often'. We do not want negative returns, certainly not across the whole portfolio. This is, of course, where diversification comes in: the share part of your portfolio may have negative returns quite often, perhaps once every four years, but the other parts (property, bonds and bank deposits) should still be producing positive returns, keeping the portfolio producing the income that you need.

Volatility risk is not about a part of your portfolio collapsing completely and permanently—that is not likely to happen to a well diversified portfolio. Rather it is a timing issue and you need to be aware of it because you want your capital to be there at the time that you want it. Investment theory suggests that a period of negative returns will not be permanent and that normal transmission, in the form of positive returns, will resume. Assuming that this is so, your risk is that your capital will not be available at certain points, that is, while you have negative returns. It may also be that your cash flow (i.e. dividends, rents and interest) also decline, which, because you are paying for the groceries from this income, is a very undesirable state of affairs.

One of the worst things that can happen to an investor is to be a seller when the markets are down. If you sell when markets are down, you crystallise a loss. Whereas if you do not sell there is still a loss, but an unrealised one. By not having to sell you are still in the market to enjoy the upside when it comes. At times this may be a long wait: occasionally shares have gone down and stayed down for a decade or more. Although this is rare, it does happen. Just as bad for those who are investing for income, a fall in the value of shares can reflect a fall in the income, profits and dividends from shares. This means that if you do not have things arranged well you can get hit by a double whammy—a fall in income and forced sale of the shares at a loss. Note also that you can make losses from both bonds and real estate as outlined in chapters 10 and 11.

If you look at the following graph, you can see the very

volatile path traced by shares against the nice smooth path traced by bank term deposits.

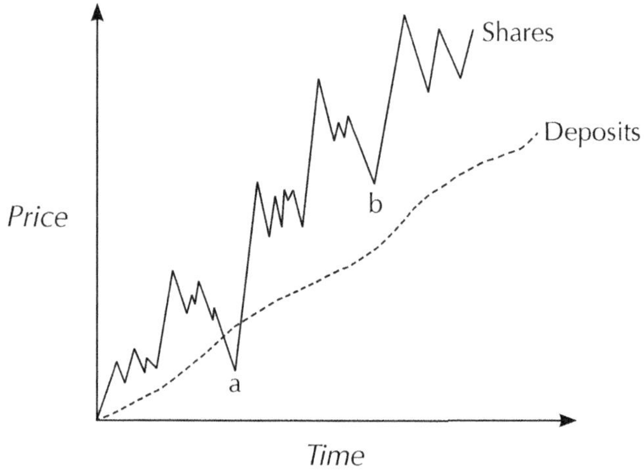

Having to sell out at points a and b is a disaster. Yet this is what happens to many people. This may be because:

- their income has fallen and so they need to dip into their capital to buy the groceries.
- they get rattled out of the market by all of the negative noise coming out of the markets through the news media.
- they need capital to replace the car or do major repairs on the home.

Volatility is why all investors have to match their portfolios to their time frames. Getting this wrong and being forced to sell out at the wrong time is one of the biggest causes of investment loss. Shares and property give the best returns but they are volatile and therefore not suitable for short-term investment as you might find that the markets are in one of their periodic down periods when you have to sell out. Two quite extreme examples illustrate this well:

1. A couple, both in their twenties, is saving for the deposit to buy their first home. This couple is best to save through bank term deposits or something similar so that the money is there when they need to buy the house.

2. A 36-year-old is saving for retirement. This person could invest in a fund or create a portfolio that is very heavily weighted towards shares and property. The value of the investment will go up and down a great deal but over the 20–30 year time frame, they are likely to see better returns than someone with a more conservative strategy.

For those investing for income in their retirement, volatility is something to be avoided as much as possible. You will not be able to avoid it completely unless you invest solely in bank deposits and that is not something that I would recommend. There are two things that you can do to lessen the impact of volatility:

1. Get the right asset allocation by diversifying your investments properly.

2. Have a pool (or lake) of cash to tide you over the rough times.

Each of these is covered in a separate chapter (see chapters 5 and 7).

Investment types and volatility

If you look at each of the investment types, each has different volatility risk characteristics. They also have different return characteristics and as the graph below indicates, the greater the expected return, the greater the volatility risk (as measured by standard deviation).

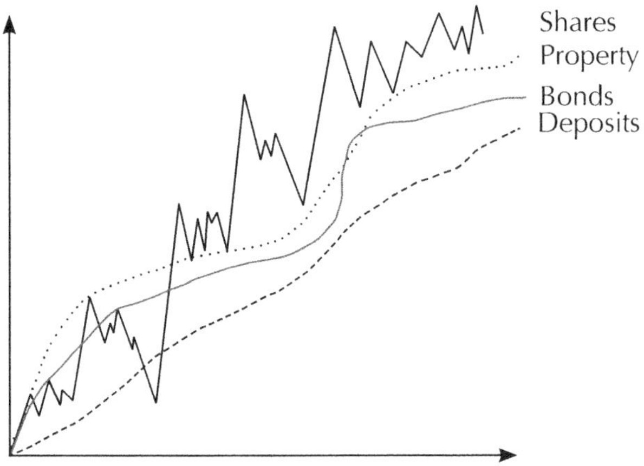

This chart is created from data that measured risk and return over the last twenty years. Sometimes, depending on the time frame that is used, one of the asset classes may step out of line and show a higher return than would be expected given a relatively low volatility. However, this is an aberration caused by the use of a relatively short time frame—in other words, during that time, this particular asset class just got lucky. If you make these measures over decades, the higher return investments show greater volatility.

Each of the main asset classes have their own risk and return characteristics.

Deposits/cash

This is the asset class with the lowest risk and the lowest returns. On the whole, people who put their money in the bank as a short-term deposit get paid a low rate of interest but they know that their money will be there when they want it. A cash deposit is thus very useful for short-term saving (i.e. less than 3 years) and to give stability to a portfolio.

It is possible to use institutions other than banks for this kind of investment. For example, you could use a finance company or a cash management trust. However, be very careful of this. Although you will get a higher return there will be a correspondingly higher risk.

It is very hard to beat banks for short-term deposits. They are supervised by a central bank and are insured to some extent. It seems to me that if you are going to have significant investments in cash deposits, they should be as safe as possible and that usually means a bank. Banks have been known to go broke, taking depositors money with them, however this is rare.

Fixed interest/bonds

These are the second least volatile investments. However, even the safest bond issued by someone who is always likely to meet its obligations (for example, a government bond) can lose money. This loss comes about when there is a rise in interest rates meaning that if you had to sell the bond to cash up, a new investor would pay less for the bond (see chapter 10). It is when bonds are tradable, and most are, that the value is readily obtainable and investors can read about profits and losses for their bonds on their computer screens or in their newspapers.

Bonds are issued by all sorts of institutions from governments, which are very safe, through to companies, which are often not very safe. Even within the different categories there are different risks—for example, a bond issued by the Australian government will be a lot safer than a bond issued by the government of Nepal; a bond issued by Coca Cola will be a lot safer than one issued by Hawes Scrap Metal Traders Ltd. Bonds are often rated by rating agencies such as Standard and Poor's, Moody's and Fitch. The biggest divide in bond ratings being between investment grade bonds and junk bonds. Not all bonds are rated and a rating does not guarantee safety. Nor is a rating any protection from volatility—even the very best bonds will fall in value when there is a rise in interest rates.

Many investors ignore the volatility of bonds by planning to hold them to maturity. The value may go up and down but providing that the issuer of the bond continues to pay the interest and is able to repay the capital on maturity, does it really matter what the value does in the meantime? Well, yes it does. This is because bonds are often for long periods of time—ten years is not uncommon and sometimes the maturity date may be even longer than that. There is quite a big chance that you will have to sell out during that time. Moreover, if interest rates rise over the period of the bond, this could be caused by a significant rise in the rate of inflation thereby making the interest that you are getting quite unattractive.

Putting aside the warning of volatility, bonds do have a very important place in the portfolios of those who are investing for twenty good summers. The volatility of bonds is not as great as the volatility of equities and there is certainty in the amount of interest you'll receive. When you buy a five-year bond, you know what interest you are going to get over that time. Provided you choose a bond from a quality issuer (e.g. a government or well-rated company) that interest will keep flowing into your bank account and your capital will be repaid on maturity. The interest that you receive will probably be greater than dividends from equities, although any capital profit will not be as big.

Property

The risks associated with property investment are interesting in that they are probably quite a lot greater than many people believe. I am a very strong advocate for property investment as a means of wealth creation. It should also be apparent to readers of this book that I also believe that property is a very important part of an income-oriented portfolio because it gives good income and some growth of both capital and income over long periods of time. However, having said this, property is not without risk and it probably does show much more volatility than you may think (see chapter 11).

Property is an excellent asset to own when you are investing for twenty good summers. It provides good income and that income is likely to grow by at least the amount of inflation. In commercial property, tenants are usually bound by long-term leases, giving security of income and, assuming that you get your exposure to commercial property via REITs, you can have a great diversity of buildings, locations, tenants and property types. Property gives the appearance of not being volatile and although that appearance may be deceptive, appearance can be reality! The appearance of having low volatility encourages people to hold property and property funds for the long haul—a very good thing. However, property investment does carry risks: the income can stop if tenants are lost and values can, and at times do, fall. While some people invest for income by buying residential property, my preference is for investors to buy into real estate trusts that are based on commercial and especially industrial property as the yields are higher, the leases longer and the income more stable.

Equities/shares

Equities are the most volatile of investments. The value of shares in companies jumps around on a second by second basis. If you have nothing else to do you can watch live trading on your computer screen and watch the value of your share portfolio change in real time. Sometimes the movements are very small, although when something happens, from the announcement of a higher than expected inflation figure to a terrorist attack, the changes can be quite dramatic. Sometimes the thing that has happened to change the share values turns out to be a false alarm and the values move back to their former levels quite quickly. At other times the news that has moved the market turns out to be real enough and the change in value becomes semi-permanent. The slightest rumour or whisper can drive the market up or down, taking the market participants' emotions with it.

It should go without saying that with shares being the most volatile asset class, it is also the highest returning asset class. Investors are always balancing risk against returns. We all want to get the highest returns, however, high returns will come with volatility—this is an immutable equation. Volatility is a very bad thing for investors who are relying on their capital to give them income on which to live. You cannot afford to have many periods when your investment returns are negative, nor can you afford to have returns that are extremely negative—that is, for the value of your portfolio to fall by 30 per cent or more. You will almost certainly get the best returns from shares over a long period of time. However, you know what would happen if you invested solely in shares. You must therefore balance the volatile part of your portfolio with some investment assets that are not volatile.

Instead of rejecting volatility risk completely, you should be thinking about how to manage it. You need to get the better returns that come from volatile assets. A big part of this is to make a conscious decision to expect volatility so that there is no surprise and then take steps to reduce its impact. For the vast majority of investors, those steps are not to simply reject property and shares as part of their portfolio, but instead to diversify widely and to make sure that you always have enough cash to tide you over during the down times that will inevitably come.

Chapter 5

Managing risk

Asset allocation

Asset allocation is simply the proportions of your investment capital that will go off to the various types of investments. Remember that there are four main asset classes—equities (shares), property, bonds (fixed interest) and cash deposits. Asset allocation means allocating certain proportions of your investment capital to each of these. Someone investing for 20 good summers will want to allocate their capital into a variety of investments so that he or she gets very wide diversification. It is the way that you allocate your investment which establishes the amount of diversification that you have.

Everything else that you do—good individual investment selection, good investment management, good timing of markets and investment will make very little difference compared to the way that you choose to allocate your assets. This is what someone who is investing for their latter years must concentrate on more than anything else. Get this wrong and twenty good summers will seem like a very long haul!

More than anything else, it is asset allocation that will dictate the returns that you will get from your capital and the volatility risk that you will experience. It is therefore the very foundation of your investment strategy. People who are investing for their retirement generally have very low risk profiles. They want to preserve the value of their investment capital and to have good steady returns. They do not want much volatility. In the past, it has been that desire for low risk investments that saw many investment advisers recommend that people investing for income invest solely in bank deposits and bonds. Although these investments are the least volatile, they do not give any capital growth, or any income growth. Growth is important for people when they start to rely on their investment capital for their income because they need to counter the insidious effects of inflation. Therefore, for most of us, investing solely in bank deposits and bonds will not provide enough income.

Given the effect that asset allocation will have on the returns that you will get and the volatility you will experience, it must be done carefully. You will also need to do it more than once. This is not something that you can do on the day that you retire and then leave for the rest of your life. Gradually, over the years, your risk profile will change. As the number of good summers reduces, you have less time and so become even more sensitive to volatility. Moreover, you will need less income and capital growth as time goes on. Therefore, your asset allocation will change over time as you reduce your exposure to equities and property and increase the amount that you have in bonds and cash deposits. A 55-year-old starting to ease back will have quite a different asset allocation to an eighty-year-old. The two people may both be retired or semi-retired but that is about all that they are likely to have in common from a financial point of view.

Asset allocation involves two things:

1. The percentage of your funds that you allocate to each of the four main investment classes: shares, property, bonds/fixed interest and cash deposits.
2. The percentage of your funds that you keep in the country where you live and the amount that you put offshore.

You will need to mix these two things together. It is not simply how much to have in shares but how much you will have in, for example, international shares and how much to have in domestic shares. This is the same with bonds, deposits and property—how much of each will you have invested locally and how much in other countries? This is important, as diversifying around different countries does lower risk. See chapter 6 for offshore investment.

Let's look now at how you should allocate your capital to the main asset classes.

Asset classes

In allocating your investment capital to the four main asset classes, you are looking to get the best return possible with reasonable or tolerable risk. There is a basic tension between growth from shares and property and stability from bonds and deposits. Each investment class shows different characteristics in its behaviour in terms of both the returns that you will get and the volatility that you are likely to experience. A good way of thinking of this is that each asset class gives something to a portfolio (perhaps high return or low risk) while each detracts from the portfolio (perhaps low returns or high volatility). Thus shares give great returns but at the price of high volatility; cash deposits give poor returns but with very low volatility.

Unfortunately, that paragon of an investment which gives high returns with low volatility risk simply does not exist. Instead, you have to piece together a portfolio that will have the characteristics that you want—a certain amount of return for a certain amount of volatility—by mixing the asset classes in certain proportions. To do this, you have to think about the risk/return characteristics of each of the four asset classes.

Cash deposits

Money held in the bank on deposit for a short period of time shows very low volatility. The capital that you put in the bank is likely to be available when you want it. This is not to say that it a risk-free investment because banks and the like have been known to go broke. If an investor kept on investing in cash deposits at banks, eventually they will take a loss and see a year of negative returns. However, that loss is likely to be a long time coming: perhaps a hundred years or longer.

This low risk of volatility is very useful because it adds stability to a portfolio. In fact, I would usually advise clients to have a higher than usual allocation to cash deposits, often at the expense of bonds. This is because a large amount of cash can act as a buffer against poor returns from other parts of your portfolio, especially shares. This buffer of cash deposits means that you know that you will always have a reasonable amount of cash available on which to live even when markets are performing poorly for extended periods. This, in turn, allows you to invest in high return/high volatility assets because having a cash buffer means other parts of your portfolio can be more heavily invested in shares and property.

The low volatility shown by cash deposits does mean that of course they will be low returning. There is always a price to pay!

Bonds

Fixed interest investments (bonds) have often been a key part of a portfolio for someone investing for income. This is because a bond pays a fixed amount of interest until maturity and so gives the investor certainty of income over that time. This is all very good provided that three conditions are met:

1. That a good quality bond is purchased and the issuer can meet the interest payments and then repay capital on maturity. There is a credit risk here. The risk is that the issuer cannot pay, which is a frequent enough occurrence. This is especially so when the bond is low quality, a so-called junk bond. My advice for most people is to stay with better rated bonds and leave the more risky ones to those people who have a bigger appetite for risk than you do. The term of a bond can be for a long period of time (ten years is not at all uncommon). Therefore there is a risk that the financial standing of the issuer can change over that time, quite possibly for the worse.

2. That you hold the bond until maturity. The value of bonds does fluctuate as interest rates change (see

chapter 10). This shouldn't be a problem provided you do not find yourself in a position where you have to sell out. If interest rates have risen, meaning your bonds are worth less than they were, you do not want to find yourself needing cash and having to sell out at a loss.

3. That there is not a lot of high inflation. If you have purchased a 10 year bond at 5 per cent the income that you will be getting towards the end of that time will buy a great deal less than at the start. Moreover, it is likely that high inflation will also drive up interest rates meaning a capital loss for your bonds. This is a double whammy leaving you in a very difficult position.

If you look at the above three conditions, you can see that there is some risk with bonds—certainly more risk than there is with cash deposits. This additional risk is the reason why long-dated bonds usually pay higher interest than short-dated cash deposits. The longer that you have your money tied up, the greater the risk (of a change to the issuers credit rating, of a change to interest rates and a change in inflation). This higher risk with longer-dated investments means that investors in bonds can demand a higher interest rate in compensation.

Property

It should be obvious to anyone who reads this book that I think property is a very good asset for those investing for income. In fact, I think it is a key asset and usually advise a higher allocation to property than many other advisers would. This is because property gives good income from rents and some capital and income growth, which should at least keep up with inflation. It also has an apparent low volatility.

This last point is important and the word that is most important in that sentence is 'apparent'. In reality, I doubt that property is really very much lower in risk than shares. Property appears to be less volatile and its value moves around a lot because property is less frequently sold. Every working day, shares in almost all listed companies are bought and sold. Every day—in fact for some companies every minute of every day—investors put their shares up for sale with the expectation that they will sell immediately. Most people selling shares are not prepared to wait for weeks and months. They want their shares are to be sold now. The price they get will depend on how many buyers there are in the market at that time.

When an investor puts a property up for sale, however, there is no expectation of a quick sale. The investor expects to have to wait weeks or months in order to sell. If the investor demanded an immediate sale, like the investor selling some shares, the property investor would have to accept the highest offer from whoever was in the market on that day. This could be good or it could be bad, depending on who was in the market. The price might be way up or way down, just like it can be with shares. The *apparent* lack of volatility is simply a timing issue brought about by the property investor's expectation of having to wait—it is probably not real at all.

Nevertheless, this appearance of low volatility caused by sellers being prepared to wait is useful enough in itself. This is because most property investors know that when they buy property that they have to be in for the long haul. It's the long haul in property that usually sees very good returns.

Nevertheless, do not be lulled into thinking that property is very low risk. If you have a liquidity problem and have to sell, you could lose money. Tenants are sometimes hard to find, especially in commercial property, and values can and do fall. I am strongly of the view that those who are investing for income later in life should diversify the property part of their portfolio and stick to the high end of the property markets. For me and my clients this usually means investing in a spread of commercial and industrial properties via managed funds. The income and growth from real estate investment trusts (REITs) along with the diversification that they offer should make them a core part of your portfolio.

Equities

Shares are the most volatile of investments. The volatility is such that it frightens many investors to the point that they refuse to invest in shares. This is a shame because although shares are high risk they are also high return and represent an excellent means to ensure your income keeps up with inflation. A good way to alleviate the fear of shares is not to think of them as ownership of shares but instead of ownership of a part of a business, which is what the shares represent. Ownership of a business often seems less scary than shares as it seems to be something more tangible.

Most people investing for income will not target 'ordinary' shares. Instead they will look for shares in companies that have steady income. These are likely to be more mature companies rather than start-ups and are quite likely to have a heavy weighting towards utility and infrastructure companies (i.e. those that supply things like electricity or water). These companies will have good dividends and, because of this, are also likely to be less volatile.

Nevertheless, any shares you own will be volatile. What will vary is the degree of volatility. There will be times when the shares that you own give a year of negative returns and, depending on the proportion of your portfolio in shares, this may put your entire portfolio into a year or more of negative returns. To increase the returns in your portfolio, this is something that you will have to face up to and manage. As shown in chapter 7, the best way to manage this is to make sure that you have a buffer of cash to allow you to continue to buy groceries while the markets are down.

Diversifying the portfolio

For most people starting to invest for income, I would suggest the following portfolio:

40–60 per cent ownership assets (shares and property)

40–60 per cent debt assets (bonds and cash deposits)

As you can see there is quite a range of possible portfolios. The performance of a portfolio which is 60 per cent in shares and property would be quite different to that of one with 40 per cent in shares and property. It is important to take this into account when building a portfolio. Age and a desire to live off investment capital are not the only factors that need to be thought about.

Other factors that need to be considered include:

- The amount of time that you are prepared to put into managing your investment portfolio. Someone who does a lot of self management is likely to be able to invest more in shares and property.
- The amount of skill that you have. The more skilled you are, the more comfortable you will be investing in shares and property.
- The amount of capital that you have. If this is marginal, you will want to put less into shares and property.
- How much you worry about money. It is not worth losing a single night's sleep worrying about your investments. If you are prone to worrying about money, build a conservative investment portfolio.

There is a benchmark that is used by some financial advisers to determine the amount of growth assets that a portfolio should contain. This works by taking 100 and then subtracting the investors age with the resulting number showing the percentage of an investor's money that should be in shares and property.

Thus, a 50-year-old would have 50 per cent in shares and property (100-50 = 50), while a 60-year-old would have 40 per cent in shares and property (100-60= 40).

I think this is an oversimplification and it does not take into account all of the factors that are listed above. It may give you something of a benchmark and it does show that age is very important in the degree to which you should diversify. However, to use a calculation like this without considering other factors would not be wise.

Some investment experts would say that 60 per cent in shares and property for someone looking for income would be very high. I have to say that a portfolio like this would be unusual. It would probably suit clients in their fifties or sixties who have continuing income from a business, job or profession and who want to continue working indefinitely. For such a person, the income derived from their investments would be only a small part of their total income.

At the other end of the spectrum, investors with 40 per cent in shares and property are likely to be older, perhaps in their 70s, or likely not to have much in the way of investment capital. There are a lot of people who are unable to tolerate any volatility because they need every dollar they can get from their investments to live on. These people would have an even lower proportion of their capital in shares and property. A downturn in investments markets of even minor proportions would mean their lifestyle would be negatively affected.

In fact, there are some people on very tight budgets who should probably have nothing in shares and property. For them everything should be in cash deposits and bonds. In fact, this portfolio should be heavily weighted towards bonds because these give certainty of income. For these people, inflation will be a major problem, but if you need every dollar of your investment returns to live on, shares and property are probably not a good idea.

That said, I would encourage most people investing for income to have a significant proportion of their portfolio in shares and property. The old days of investing solely in bonds and deposits are largely gone because people tend to be retired for longer.

Now, more than in the past, there is additional risk when you have bigger amounts of shares and property as the volatility will be greater. This can be managed by diversifying widely. You can diversify by investing in:

- different industries
- different companies
- different fund managers
- different countries

It is when you end up with a high exposure to just one country or just one fund manager that things can get very difficult. For example, I have known investors who have thought that they were well diversified because they had investments in several managed funds that were based in different countries and asset classes. However, all of the funds were with just one manager and the loss of key staff meant that this manager's performance slipped badly. Diversifying widely will mean that you have a lot of relatively small investments which will increase the amount of management that you have to do. Quite simply, this is the price that you have to pay for proper diversification.

Investing in a range of different asset classes and investment types is the smart thing to do to manage volatility. You could manage volatility by simply investing in low risk investments. The problem with this is that they will all be low return. By combining a range of investments, you can get the best of both worlds. (In his book *Against the Gods—the remarkable story of risk,* Peter L Bernstein calls this diversification the closest thing that an investor can ever get to a free lunch).

As far as possible you want to combine different investments whose returns do not correlate. By this I mean that the ideal is for you to own investments that do not all go up at the same time or down at the same time. For example, bonds do not tend to go up in value when shares do. This is because bonds are a good investment when interest rates are falling. When interest rates fall it is usually because the economy has weakened, which is a bad time for shares. Conversely, in the part of the economic cycle when interest rates are rising, the economy is most likely to be strong. This is good for shares and bad for bonds. Bonds and shares have a negative correlation—when one is going up the other will be going down. This negative correlation will not be perfect. There will be times when bonds and shares move in the same direction together but this is unusual. Nevertheless, owning both bonds and shares will smooth out the volatility in your portfolio and they are good assets to hold together.

It actually gets better than this. If you combined two investment assets, say some bonds and some shares, in a portfolio you would expect that you would get a return that reflects the average return of bonds and shares. At the same time, you would expect to experience an amount of volatility equivalent to the average volatility of shares and bonds. In fact it does not work like this at all: because of a quirk of mathematics (as it was described an actuary friend of mine) you end up getting a return that is a little *better* than the average of the two investments, and at the same time experience *less* volatility than would be expected. The combining of different investment assets within a portfolio (i.e. diversification) actually adds to your return while reducing risk. It may sound too good to be true but it was this that won Harry Markowitz the Nobel Prize (and the Swedes do not usually give these out unless there is some fairly good science behind the thinking). This is called the 'efficient frontier' and is the basis for modern portfolio theory.

So, diversification, combining investment assets with a negative correlation, adds to your returns and at the same time reduces risk. No wonder that Bernstein called it the nearest thing to a free lunch!

Remember that although there are only four main asset classes, each of these can be broken down almost to infinity. For example, we consider shares as one asset class. However, within that class there are shares from different industries (transport, mining, infrastructure, etc) and from different countries (domestic or international, emerging markets or developed markets, Asia and Europe). It is not enough to simply combine asset classes—you should be thinking of combining individual investments which are not too much in sync. For example, if you already have significant investments in Asia, it wouldn't be a good idea to have too much invested in Australian mining companies (e.g. BHP or Rio Tinto) because their success comes from the growth in Asia. If Asian economies strike tough times, the chances are that BHP and Rio Tinto would also strike trouble.

The more negative correlations that you can find among your investments—the more investments that you can find which are likely to be out of sync with each other—the better your portfolio will be, meaning higher returns and lower volatility. Nirvana for investors.

Chapter 6 Get offshore

Another important part of asset allocation and diversification is ensuring that you put some investment outside of the country where you live. A strategy of investing offshore is the ultimate form of diversification because you are then diversifying across economies and countries as well as asset classes and industries.

There is still some disagreement among investment experts regarding the amount that you should diversify offshore. There are investment advisers who believe that you should have very little offshore. Their main arguments appear to be twofold:

1. Your liabilities are in the country where you live. By this they mean that you have to buy the groceries and fund your other living costs in your domestic currency and if you have a great deal of your wealth in other currencies you may take a currency loss through exchange rate movements that would result in a reduction in lifestyle. This argument does have some validity—you should be matching your liabilities with your assets as far as possible and having investments in other currencies means that you are not doing that.

2. You know your domestic market better and therefore will make better investments there rather than in the unknown foreign ones. This also has some validity but only for active do-it-yourself investors, who have more information and therefore a better feel for their domestic markets. However, those who invest via managed funds are paying someone else to do the investing for them and should be less bothered about where the investments are.

There are other experts who believe that a very high proportion should go offshore. These experts would go as far as saying that those living in small countries with limited economies should have all of their wealth offshore. Their arguments are:

1. You get better diversification by having investments in a wide range of countries. This should almost go without saying and is the primary reason why you should have at least some of your investment capital offshore.

2. You can access other industries and other companies by investing offshore. This increases the range of opportunities that you have as all countries have industries, and therefore investments that are specific to them. Some countries are stronger in certain areas (for example, the USA is very strong in technology) making them better areas to invest in.

When you line up the thoughts from both sides of this argument, it seems to me to be obvious that you should have some of your money offshore. However, unless you live in the Solomon Islands or Swaziland, not all of your investments should be offshore—you should retain some for domestic investment.

How much offshore?

Looking at the arguments for both sides, I believe that most people should have 40–60 per cent of their portfolios offshore. By doing this, they can get the best of all worlds:

1. They have a good proportion of their money domestically which will cover, at least in part, their living costs.
2. You can be an active investor with the money that you have domestically but use managed funds for exposure to offshore markets. This is my own strategy: I select and buy investments in Australia and New Zealand as these are markets of which I have some knowledge. However, I use managed funds for exposure to the USA and Europe and to emerging markets (especially Asia) as they are markets that I do not know well.
3. Having 40–60 per cent offshore gives you good diversification. You no longer have all of your eggs in the domestic market. You have exposure to other currencies and economies, which spreads your risk around the world.
4. There are opportunities that are not available if you restrict yourself to domestic investments. This may

be global brands (American Express or Vodafone) or whole industries (greentech or biotech).

When you look at this in its totality, there is a compelling case for getting some money offshore. However, it should not all go offshore:

1. You will need to buy the groceries with domestic currency and a major shift upwards in your currency against other currencies that you invest in will make it harder to do that. Some years ago I had some friends who moved all their quite considerable wealth offshore. They were convinced that the currency was as high as it was going to get and it was therefore a good time to do this. In fact, the currency moved against them as the dollar rose in value. This couple was reduced to bringing back $4000 each month to pay for groceries as they hoped for a fall in the value of the dollar. As I write, that fall still has not happened!

2. There is complication in investing offshore because you do not know it as well. This means that you become quite reliant on managed funds, which is not attractive to many people.

Hence, I think that 40-60 per cent offshore is about right. The amount that you choose between 40 per cent and 60 per cent depends on some other factors. These factors are:

1. The amount of overseas travel that you have in your lifestyle plans. The more travel you intend to do,

the more money that you should have in overseas investments as a hedge against the costs of your travel rising because of foreign exchange fluctuations. If you have one or two countries that you expect to travel to more than any other, it is the assets and currencies of these countries that you should invest in (provided that they are not the Solomon Islands or Swaziland). For example, if you expect to spend six weeks each year in Italy and France, I would strongly suggest that you have some investments that are denominated in Euros and also had some Euros in cash in a bank so that if the Euro strengthens, you will still be able to afford to live in France or Italy. This would result in you having more offshore than you otherwise might. You might not use the returns from the investments to fund your stay overseas, however, if you have the investments there, the natural hedge works because major changes in value to currency or investment should be a reflection of what is going on in the country. For example, Ireland has done extremely well over the last fifteen years. (Joan and I travel to Ireland for work and family reasons every year.) Because the economy in Ireland has boomed, everything has become extremely expensive. However, we have had investments in Ireland and as you would expect these have done very well. The good performance of these investments means that I can still stand my round at the pub on Saturday nights.

2. Active investors should have less allocated to

offshore investments. They are likely to get better returns onshore as they use their skills and abilities to move money around quickly, taking advantage of opportunities as they arise. If you are really confident that you have the skills to actively invest well, you will probably want to allocate more of your capital at home. And, of course, the area where you will be most successful in active management is onshore not offshore.

3. The country where you live will also be a factor. If you live in a small country with a quite brittle economy (think Solomon Islands or Swaziland) you should have virtually no assets invested domestically. On the other hand, if you live in the USA or the UK you should have correspondingly more. The Solomon Islands and Swaziland may be wonderful places to live but that does not mean that you should have much invested there. The USA or the UK are big diversified economies and although you will not want to have everything invested there, you should be reasonably safe having a higher proportion of your funds at home.

Investing offshore

There are two things that you need to be mindful of when investing offshore and both of them can add to or detract from your investment performance. The first of these things is the chance (in fact, the certainty) of currency movements. These are notoriously difficult to pick. Although you can look at a currency and say that it is under- or over-valued, when it will move to a fair value can be anyone's guess. Sometimes currencies can remain mispriced for years. Because of the currency fluctuation, I think that offshore investment should almost always be done by dollar cost averaging (see chapter 9). This means making your offshore investments slowly. I have seen people take big investment losses because they have invested all of their cash at one time. This is especially dangerous with offshore investing because you can take a double hit on both the currency and the investment markets.

Currency is quite volatile and its movements can be quite large over a year or two. However, over long periods of time the value of any particular currency is likely to reflect the strength of that country's economy. My best advice on the currency aspect of offshore investments is not to be reactive to events, but instead to take a long-term view. The last thing that you want to do is to sell out of a particular currency because it has been falling. If you do that you are likely to be selling the currency into weakness.

It is good to be able to profit from currency movements if you can, however do not fall into the trap of becoming some kind of de facto currency trader. You should have a number of different currencies because you should have invested across several different countries. Investing in a number of different countries and currencies along with taking a long-term view will mean that over time currency movements will even themselves out.

The second thing that affects your overall investment performance is the performance of the individual investments themselves. This is likely to be much more important than the fluctuations in the value of currencies, especially in the long term.

When you put currency movements and the performance of the investments themselves together you can get times when you get stellar performance or performance that makes you want to sell out. When the currency and the investment both go up in value it is fantastic; when they both go down together it can be disastrous. When one goes up and one goes down performance will be neither disastrous nor fantastic but it can nevertheless seem frustrating because one seems to be holding the other back. The two aspects, currency and investment performance, can mean a good deal of additional volatility that you have to cope with when you look at individual investments. However, a spread of investments across different countries and different asset classes should smooth out this volatility. In any event, there will be less volatility than if you were to only invest domestically.

Having said that, you have to be aware there is a growing trend towards a greater correlation of investments around the world. By this I mean that more and more, investments move in sync. If one major market moves, all of the others tend to move in the same direction. This is the genesis of the saying that when the USA sneezes the rest of the world catches a cold. Improved communications and more freedom to move money around the world have resulted in this closer correlation. Clearly this makes diversification more difficult (and a bit less effective). However, it does not negate the basic principle that you ought to diversify beyond the country where you live.

Passive or active investing?

For the vast majority, the offshore part of the portfolio should be by way of managed funds. This passive approach to investment is right for offshore assets because most people do not have the necessary inside knowledge of the markets. I encourage people to take direct management of the domestic parts of their portfolios, assuming that they have the aptitude, skills, motivations and a desire to learn. However, I am wary of people taking a do-it-yourself approach to offshore investment. It is true that information is now much more readily available and that you can place buy or sell orders for shares or bonds very easily. However, unless you are prepared to spend a great deal of time reading and watching the markets you will be unlikely to get an investment performance as good as the average.

The average in any market, whether it is for certain kinds of bonds or shares or property, is represented by an index. It is very easy to invest in index tracking funds (see chapter 9) and, because these attract very low fees, they tend to give returns very close to the index. It seems to me that because it easy to achieve an average performance, and quite difficult and risky to try to beat the average, most people should be satisfied with the average for their offshore holdings. It is unlikely that you have any particular skills or knowledge that would mean you are able to beat the market in another country. Therefore, be happy with the average and invest most of your offshore money via index trackers.

This idea of settling for the average may sound a bit negative to some people and I stress that it is only for the offshore parts of your portfolio. However, there are some people who simply will not accept average in anything that they do—even offshore investment. If you are one of these people, you may want to try to enhance your returns by adopting a strategy whereby you invest most of your offshore allocations via passive index tracking funds but retain some of your funds to invest outside of the index. This may mean that you invest 80 per cent of your offshore equities allocation in index trackers and use the other 20 per cent of the funds to invest in special opportunities or companies.

For example, you may use some of the 20 per cent retained to buy some shares in Warren Buffett's company, Berkshire Hathaway, or invest in some other actively managed fund that has a record of out-performance over a long period of time. These 'kickers' ought to enhance your returns, although if you get it wrong they will detract from them. If you invest in these with a relatively small part of your investment capital, you will never be too far away from the average performance.

This is a strategy that I adopt personally—I always try to beat the average. It is something that has, on the whole, been successful for me and I have invested in things as varied as Google shares, a pharmaceutical managed fund and a company which owned a portfolio of Singaporean industrial property. Not all of these were brilliantly successful but overall they have added to returns and have also provided a good bit of interest and even, at times, excitement.

To get as much diversification as possible, you should invest offshore in each of the four asset classes. If possible do not invest in just two or three of them. Try to get exposure across the board:

Cash deposits

This is usually managed most easily by having foreign currency accounts with your local bank. Nearly all banks offer these across a wide variety of currencies. Holding some foreign currency as a bank deposit is a good idea for those who want to travel, although it may be more convenient to open a bank account in a country if you travel there regularly. You may, at times, also want to hold currency that you are going to use in the future when you make other offshore investments.

I often suggest to clients who are going to make substantial investments offshore that they open foreign currency accounts with their bank and hold these funds for some time. This is usually at a time when it seems advantageous to move money offshore as a result of attractive exchange rates. Buying the currency by opening a foreign currency bank account means that you have covered that part of offshore investment—you will then dollar cost average into specific investments over some years (see page 126).

Bonds

I do not recommend buying individual offshore bonds but instead think it better that you invest via bond managed funds. There are lots of these, both passive and actively managed, which can give you exposure to many different fixed interest markets. It should be noted that one of the best performing investments for several years was Emerging Markets bonds. At one time these attracted very high interest rates but when the market re-assessed the risk, the interest rates came down which resulted in very large capital profits for investors. There are some very good actively managed bond funds around the world, however these are not easy to pick and given the higher fees that such funds charge, you are probably better to put most of your money into passive index trackers.

Property

There are many real estate investment trusts (REITs) around the world and they are generally easy to invest in. Few of us have enough money to buy individual properties ourselves and even those who do are usually better to get their exposure to international property via managed funds. Investing in REITs gives you better diversification and allows you to invest in much better property. Do not invest in just one REIT—you need to diversify management risk as well as diversify into different countries and different property types.

Shares

There are thousands and thousands of different shares and it is easy to be confused by the vast array and competing commercial claims of many of them. My advice is to keep things simple by investing in two or three index tracking funds based on the main markets (Europe and the USA) with smaller amounts in tracker funds based in more specialised areas like emerging markets and perhaps a special industry or two (e.g. biotech or greentech).

Offshore investment is an area where nearly everyone needs good advice. I stress the need to invest money offshore but I do acknowledge that it can be difficult. It is important to get the diversification that offshore investment gives and to take advantage of the opportunities that are afforded by looking at everything that is offered around the world; however, it is in this area where I have seen the most investment losses. Get some money offshore but go slowly and carefully, with good advice.

Chapter 7 Managing risk

Lakes and rivers

You must be ready for volatility and as such need to arrange your money so that you always have ready cash. Holding a good amount of cash at all times is critical if you are to be able to meet your expenses on an ongoing basis. Therefore you need to smooth out the investment returns that you get by putting in a buffer. I see this as a lake (or reservoir) of cash. In good times, the returns from your investments will flow into the lake raising the level; in bad times you are then able to draw on the reservoir that you have created thereby lowering its level. Having this lake that controls and buffers the flow of returns means that you do not have to sell your core investments (bonds, shares and property) during the bad times. For older investors, volatility can be a killer and wreck lives. If your money is not well arranged and you do not have enough cash, volatility can turn you into a forced seller, just at the time when you should not be selling.

For a young person, volatility is not a great problem. People in their twenties, thirties, forties and sometimes in their fifties can tolerate a lot of volatility because they have no need for their savings as they have their jobs to give them their day to day incomes. They also have time for the markets to rectify a major downturn with the major upturn that will eventually follow. These factors mean that younger people can afford to be very heavily weighted towards shares and property. The volatility shouldn't bother them and they know that they will get higher returns over time.

However, people who are dependent on their investments to give them income so that they can get on with enjoying a limited number of summers are in a completely different position. They cannot tolerate volatility. The ups and downs can wreck their lives, ruining every dream and plan that they had for their later years.

Volatility is a life wrecker. Markets are cyclical—good times follow bad times and vice versa. The worst thing that can happen is for you to become a forced seller—that is, to be in a position where you have to sell investments regardless of whether it is a good time or a bad time (it is almost always bad times that people sell into).

People can and do get caught in bad economic times: their returns are down and so they have to sell out of some investment and use the capital to live on. They get poor prices for the investments that they sell and therefore have less capital when the market starts to rise again. Worse, many people will have nothing in certain markets because they have been forced to sell. They are out of the market and so do not enjoy the upturn when it eventually comes.

There is some simple mathematics that you need to be aware of: a relatively small fall in the markets needs a much bigger rise to put you back to the same position. If you had a 20 per cent fall in one of your investments, you would need a 25 per cent rise to be back to your starting point. For example, if you had $100,000 in shares and they fell by 20 per cent, you would have $80,000. To restore the value of your shares, you would need a 25 per cent rise in the market to get back to $100,000. You must avoid selling into downturns. You do not want to crystallise your losses. Nor do you want to sell into the bottom of a market slump because you will not then enjoy the bounce back when it comes.

For young people a year or two of poor or negative returns should not be of concern. Provided they do not get rattled out of the market by the negative noise, the markets will eventually come right. A young person should actually welcome volatility as it gives opportunities. For older people, volatility will see your lifestyle affected—you will have to start to reuse those tea bags—and you should avoid it as much as possible, being prepared for what you cannot avoid. It is important, therefore, that you not listen to a great deal of the investment advice in the media. This is largely aimed at younger investors and does not necessarily apply to you.

There is an old investment saying: *buy in gloom, sell in boom*. It is very easy to say (and to write), but much harder to do. In fact, most people do exactly the opposite. They buy when markets are booming and end up selling when markets are gloomy. They sell either because of the wall of negative noise that comes out of the markets or because they have to cash up to be able to pay the bills. Whichever it is, selling into gloom is a disaster and it is something that you must avoid.

You must have volatility

Although you do not want volatility, you need to have it. This is because volatility means that you will get higher returns.

As I have said, the alternative to volatility is investing in areas which will give very low returns, such as bank deposits. Few of us have enough money to be able to accept such low returns so we have to increase our volatility risk. You should try to diversify out this volatility as far as you possibly can—but you will still have to be prepared for ups and downs.

Remember that investment risk is defined as the amount by which an investment deviates from the expected returns. These deviations can be on both the upside and the downside. Sometimes an investment will provide returns that are superior and sometimes returns that are inferior. In fact, with most investments returns seldom fit neatly on the average, and if they do, it is only for short periods of time.

Given that your portfolio is likely to always have either unders or overs from what is expected and that you need consistency to pay for the groceries, how do you manage your money and investments to always have the cash that you require to live?

A buffer

My answer to this is to put in a buffer (a lake or reservoir) between your investment capital and your expenditure. This buffer takes the form of a bank account that is interest bearing but that is either on call or at least can be drawn on at fairly short notice (no more than 90 days). As such this bank account represents a good part (possibly even all) of the allocation that you make to cash deposits.

Ideally, this buffer account would hold an amount equivalent to at least a year of expenditure—preferably it would hold an amount sufficient to live on for two years.

Of course, not everyone will have this sort of cash but the thinking behind it is that the buffer account will mean that you do not have to sell investments to live on when times get tough. If you have two years worth of expenditure in an account, you can draw on that money when markets are down, which would be the worst time to sell. It is unlikely that your overall portfolio will show negative returns for more than two years, although it could if you are very aggressively invested. An amount of cash equivalent to two years of expenditure should give you a great deal of comfort and allow you to sit out the bad times. You will not, then, have to be a forced seller.

A lake and a river

The buffer account really works like putting a dam across a river. Imagine a river running unimpeded from its source in the mountains to the sea. When it rains, the river rises and if it rains a lot you get a deluge. When it does not rain and there is a drought, the river dries up. With an unimpeded river, rain goes straight into the river and the flow increases immediately. This is the same with your investments: when times are good you have a great deluge of returns coming into your account ready to spend; when times are bad nothing comes in and you can't pay the bills.

If, however you put a dam across the river, a lake will form. Water will run into this lake and the dam will control the amount of water coming out. Great deluges from heavy rain can be stored in the lake. The lake level will rise but the flow of water in the river can be maintained. When there is a drought, you can continue to take water out as you draw on the lake's storage capacity. The level of the lake will lower but you will still have water to draw on because, unless there's a terrible drought, the lake will always have water in it.

Having a buffer bank account acts like a lake, allowing you a constant amount on which to live. Without the financial equivalent of a lake, you are dependent on regular rainfall. You have no reservoir to draw on when returns dry up.

Most financial planning literature says that you should hold cash reserves of an amount equivalent to three months spending. However, this benchmark is for younger people, those who are likely to be working. Those of us who are dependent upon our investment capital should have more cash as a reserve— at least one year and preferably two years. The reason for this is that in a severe market downturn, you could have negative returns for a year or possibly longer. You want to be able to live off this reserve while you wait for investment returns to normalise. Provided that you have a reasonably well diversified portfolio, your overall returns should not be negative for longer than that. If they are, the world has real economic problems! The last thing that you want is to be forced to sell into such a market downturn.

Note that this reserve fund is not simply something to be drawn on when times are bad. In fact, the cash that you have in this account acts as a buffer, smoothing out returns in good times and bad. We all know that investment returns never come consistently and smoothly—there are always ups and downs. It is important that during good times returns go into this buffer account and are not spent, meaning that your spending should remain constant regardless of what your returns are. In my experience, buoyant times are nearly as dangerous as hard times. Long periods of strong investment returns are great—we all enjoy them. However, they can lead to thoughts and feelings which themselves lead to trouble. For example:

- My investment returns are fantastic. This investment game is easy.
- I have had good returns now for several years. This will carry on forever.
- We have more money now than we thought that we would have. Let's have another trip overseas.
- Our returns from shares have been great. Let's put more into the market.

Dealing with market booms is as important as dealing with busts. Booms are a time to salt away the additional returns that you are getting. When a boom lasts several years, it is a great danger to assume that the markets will always be like this. Such hubris leads to higher spending and a lack of reserves. Eventually, booming markets will revert to the norm—there will be a bust. You need plenty salted away to continue to live through the bust.

As you sit and read this, you know that the investment game is not easy, that strong markets do not continue forever, that you cannot spend more than you have budgeted for and that you should not move beyond your asset allocation limits. Of course, you may know this at the moment, but every day people get caught up in the emotional whirl of the markets and do things that they know, at least in hindsight, that they should not do.

It is important that super returns or returns above what was expected are put away against the poor returns that will come when the markets revert to the norm. In fact, I usually suggest to clients that they structure their affairs so that all investment returns go into the buffer account and that the required amount comes out of the buffer each month to cover living expenses. This is the only way that I can think of to smooth out investment returns, to be sure that you will have enough to live on and to make sure that you neither fall to the hubris that comes from success nor get panicked out of the market when times get tough. This, along with regularly rebalancing of your portfolio, should ensure that you will have the money that you want and expect.

Having this buffer account means that not only will the returns from both good and bad times be smoothed out but returns that are irregular will also be smoothed. Most investments pay interest or dividends regularly. Although the payments for each may be regular, the time period varies, some pay monthly, others quarterly and some may pay out every six months. A lot of people depending on their investment capital to pay for their living expenses find this difficult as most supermarkets are not very interested in providing groceries on the basis that the dividend cheque from Rio Tinto is coming in a couple of months. The reservoir which is your buffer account smooths this irregular cash flow as well.

Buffer account

Everyone should have a buffer account to act as a lake on the river that is the flow of your investment returns. All income should come in to the buffer account and an amount that has been established by doing a budget should come out regularly by automatic payment.

There are several things you should remember when establishing a buffer account:

- Make sure that it is interest bearing. Many banks now pay quite high interest on call accounts, especially if you keep to their minimum balance requirements and use internet banking.
- Have at least one year and preferably two years of expenditure in it. If you have income from sources that are not your investment capital and that are secure, such as superannuation payments, this can be deducted from the amount that you need to have in the account.
- Make sure that all your investment returns go into the account and that only the budgeted amount comes out.
- Use the buffer account to live on. Try not to sell out of investments when the markets are down.

Having a lake into which the river of your investment returns flow is a very important part of money management for those investing for income. Your lumpy and uneven investment returns go into the account and a nice smooth flow will come out. This should remove the temptation of overspending in good times and allow you to keep spending when the markets are not performing.

Chapter 8 Managing your investments

One of the major issues that you will have to address and resolve early on is the amount of time, effort and energy that you are willing to put into the management of your investments. This is an important issue because it can affect both your lifestyle and the returns that you get. The worst-case scenario is that you put a lot into active management of your investments, and this uses up a lot of your time, creating stress and leaving you with poor returns. I have seen this happen to people frequently. On the other hand, and more positively, I have seen people manage their own investments, love the challenge, intellectual stimulation and engagement of investment management and get very good returns.

All else being equal, I would prefer people to take advice but to invest directly themselves rather than using managed funds. I also think they should manage their own investments. This is not to say that managed funds do not have their place. I use managed funds for my investments in commercial property (real estate investment trusts) and for much of my offshore investment (especially in emerging markets like China and India). Nevertheless, I think that people should be in charge of their own affairs and not be completely reliant on professionals. Professional advisers give advice, and can make investment decisions for you. They may also act as custodians of your portfolio. You must always remember, however, that this is your money and I do not think that you should completely remove yourself from its management. I recognise that there are people who have no interest in or aptitude for investment. They need to make sure that they use the very best advisers and managers available to them.

If you do not want to manage your investments yourself, there are any number of companies who will do it for you. They charge, of course, and their costs will eat into your returns. I believe that you will be better off having taken good advice and then doing as much as you can yourself. Nevertheless, using money managers in some form or other is right for many people.

There are two aspects for you to consider when thinking about investment management:

1. Whether you invest directly into shares, bonds or property, or whether you use managed funds.
2. Whether you look after your own portfolio or have someone else do that for you. There are firms who act as custodians and will hold your investments in their own name, reporting to you regularly and giving you a tax statement each year.

Advice is, of course, a quite separate matter. I think that all investors, no matter how skilled, should have an investment adviser who they can talk to regularly.

Management of investments

You should see the degree of investment management as a spectrum with extremes on each end and on which we all fit somewhere.

At the passive end of the spectrum is an investor who hands everything over to a money manager. This money manager invests the money (largely in managed funds or equities) and provides the investor with a monthly (or quarterly) cheque representing the returns from the portfolio. The manager will also give a regular report to the investor or even to the investor's accountant when the investor is very passive. All of this means that the investor is not involved at all in investment strategy and decisions or the day to day management of their money. This allows the investor to get on with the things that they want to do without having to put any time into deriving income from capital—a cheque appears every period available to be spent. There is a cost for this and with this amount of management the cost is likely to be high. This approach doesn't necessarily guarantee a worry-free life: the investment strategy and execution of that strategy is only ever going to be as good as the manager's competence and trustworthiness. At this end of the spectrum finding a very good manager is absolutely vital.

At the other end of the spectrum, the investor looks after everything. They set the investment strategy and asset allocation, identify and invest in particular investments, monitor the value and performance of the investments, bank the dividend or interest cheques, fill in the tax forms and all of the other daily minutiae that is inevitably involved. This end of the spectrum is very active and such people tend to shun managed funds and other managed investments. It does take a great deal of time. However a lot of people regard their work on their investments as either part of their paid employment because they are saving money on managers' fees or as an interesting and engaging hobby.

Most of us fit somewhere more towards the middle of this spectrum. Very few of us are completely passive and hand over our investment capital to be looked after by a professional. Similarly not many of us look after all aspects of our investments ourselves. Most of us buy in some professional help, whether that is an accountant for tax, a full-service share broker or investment adviser. Your task is to work out where you want to fit on this spectrum on the basis of how interested you are and the skills that you have.

In general, I try to encourage people to be as active in their investments as their skills allow. I personally find the world of investment fascinating as it takes in just about everything that is going on in society: politics, scientific advancement, economics, history and so on. Good investors keep their eyes on all of these things because they really need to know what opportunities and threats exist. I love to watch these things and to see how they play out in the performance of particular investments, although I am prepared to admit that not everyone has the same fascination with this stuff that I do.

In deciding where you fit on the spectrum, skills are not the only factors. One of the most important factors is quite personal: you have to actually want to be involved. I am always fairly careful when dealing with a client that I do not impose my love of the investment game onto someone who really wants to get on with other things. I believe that money management should make a nice fit with the way that you want to live your life and that there is no point shoehorning you into something that is really quite unsuitable for you. You may have all of the skills that are necessary to learn about investment and can perhaps see that there are good savings to be made by doing it yourself rather than using a financial planning firm and other managers. Nevertheless, if you are not comfortable, you are not comfortable—and your level of comfort and desire to spend time doing what you enjoy is more important than mere money. If managing your money is a chore and is stopping you from enjoying your summers, a passive investment approach is for you.

To decide where you want to sit on the active versus passive investment spectrum, it is useful to look at what the management of investment requires. There are four main tasks:

1. **Setting the investment strategy.** For the most part, this is establishing the asset allocation as other areas, like gearing or borrowing to buy investments, are largely irrelevant to people who are investing later in life. Asset allocation is an important aspect of setting your investment strategy because it, more than anything else, will determine what returns you get and the amount of volatility you experience. In my experience, most people need help with this. I frequently see people whose asset allocation is poor with far too much, sometimes everything, in one asset—perhaps in corporate bonds or residential property. Asset allocation is a major theme of this book because it is the foundation of any investment

strategy. It is critical that you get it right—if you are going to pay for help in just one area, this is it.

2. **Investment selection.** Once you have the asset allocation right you will need to identify good investments in each asset area. For example, if your asset allocation required you to have $100,000 in international equities, you will need to find either the individual shares or the best managed funds to give you exposure to this market. It is hard to pick the right particular international shares. For example, if you want to invest in a bank, do you buy CitiGroup or HSBC? Some people manage this themselves but in my experience they are few in number—those who do it well are few in number anyway. Most people will want to get their exposure to these kinds of markets via managed funds (unit trusts and the like). However, even that is difficult without undertaking a lot of top-flight research. How do you know which particular managed fund will perform the best? Research has shown that if you pick a managed fund that has been outperforming the others for the past few years, it is likely to return to the norm soon and start having some bad years. One school of thought says that you should buy the worst performing trust on the basis that it is likely to return to the norm and start outperforming the others. This is not something I would recommend to do blindly, even though there is some logic in it. The answer is to use an investment adviser to help with the selection of trusts. This investment adviser is

likely to buy in research from one of the big research houses (for example, Morningstar and Fundsource) and should therefore know the more highly rated funds. The other solution is to use passive index tracker funds. The thing is to make a decision as to whether you are going to try to pick individual investments yourself (and if so with whose help) or whether you will tend more towards managed funds.

3. **Monitoring investments.** You cannot simply set and forget your investments. Perhaps (and I emphasise the 'perhaps') a young person could do that: buy a bundle of good shares and forget them for twenty years while they grow. However, someone investing for income for twenty summers definitely has to monitor and keep monitoring their investments. The risk in this is that you become overly reactive. That is, when the markets move you buy or sell. Nevertheless, there are times when you do have to sell, especially when markets are booming. This can and does happen in any market: shares, property and bonds. Monitoring involves three functions:

    i. The continual weeding out of poorly performing investments. Again you have to be careful with this. Try not to do the weeding just before the apparent weed changes into a beautiful flower. Do not look back at past performance but try to look ahead. If the investment case is still valid, be patient. If something has changed, forget about what you paid for the investment: sell it and get your money (albeit depleted) working better elsewhere. Never worry about what you paid for an investment as that is in the past. It is the future that is important.

ii. The continual quest for new opportunities. Again you have to be careful of this. The Casanova syndrome means that some investors are continually look for the new and exciting investment when, in fact, the best investments are already tucked up safe and snug in their portfolio. This can mean that, like Casanova, you get rid of something really good to chase something that may turn out to be no better. Nevertheless, new and better opportunities do come along and you should not be blindly faithful to the old investments that you own.

iii. Rebalancing. At times your asset allocation can get away from what it should be. This could be because there has been some movement in a market which has meant that a certain asset class has risen or fallen. For example, you may be meant to have an allocation of 40 per cent to bonds. Over a couple of years, the value of your bonds has risen because of a fall in interest rates and so bonds now make up 55 per cent of your portfolio. You should sell some of your bonds to bring the allocation to bonds down to correct levels, investing the funds from the sale into an asset class that has less invested in it than what was supposed to be allocated. This needs to be a continual process. If you do not do it, the effect can be disastrous. A major crash in bond values when you have 55 per cent of your portfolio in them will be much more serious than if you have 40 per cent in bonds. You need to keep the amount invested in each asset class close to the percentages of asset allocations you set when you began investing for your twenty good summers.

The other part of rebalancing is that as you get older you can change the target asset allocation. Someone starting to ease back into semi-retirement may have a life expectancy of 30 years and so need quite a high exposure to property and equities to keep up with inflation. However, as time goes on the investor can lower the allocation to property and shares, perhaps after a decade the 40 per cent allocation to property and shares might be lowered to 30 per cent with more put in bonds and deposits.

4. **Administration.** This is something that many people hate. The minutiae of banking dividend and interest cheques, record keeping and filing, filling in forms and so on drive a lot of people mad. Sure, there are some people who actually enjoy the detail, but not many. Although you may not like this sort of thing very much, have a good think before you contract it out to professional management. The big advantage in doing the administration of your investments yourself is that you get a good feel for what is going on. You see interest, rents and dividends come in. You get the notices of meetings and annual reports

and you listen to the tenants' complaints. Yes, it's a chore but at least you know what is happening.

You can contract any or all of these things out if that is what you want to do. Work out which parts you are good at, which parts you are prepared to learn and which parts you actively enjoy. Think about where a professional can add value to your situation and where they are likely to be a cost with little benefit to yourself.

Finally, a warning: no professional who takes up a part or all of the management of your investments will care as much about them as you do. No professional will go home at 5pm after a day at the office and carry on worrying about your particular investments. This is not to say that they don't care, they do, but they will never care as much as you do.

Managed funds

Managed funds come under a lot of different names: unit trusts, syndicates, mutual funds, investment trusts. However, they all work in much the same way: a manager promotes the investment to investors who pool their money for it to be invested in a particular area. A trustee holds the funds in the trustee's name but it is the manager who makes all the decisions within the agreed mandate. There are, of course, thousands of managed funds available, promoted by different banks, insurance companies and fund managers, and based on many different investment markets. If you want exposure to a particular area, whether it is gold, greentech, retail property or Asian shares, there is a selection of many different funds that you can use.

While I generally like people to invest directly themselves, there are a lot of instances where this is not practicable. It may be that the investor simply does not have the skills to choose investments or it may be that he or she wants to invest in some difficult area like an emerging market or oil prospecting. As I have already mentioned, I use managed funds for investing in China and India. I recognise these countries, especially China, as excellent places to invest. They have had quite astonishing growth over the last twenty years and this growth does not look like it is going to stop any time soon. However, I do not know which area of China to invest in, what companies are best, how the financial and tax system works and I know nothing of the legal environment. I cannot read Mandarin, which means I would struggle to even be able read a dividend statement let alone an annual report, assuming that they have such things in China. Therefore, I invest in these kind of places via managed funds. That is, I effectively pay experts in the area to invest for me.

I use a similar approach with commercial property. I have always preferred commercial property to residential property but do not have the tens or hundreds of millions of dollars that are required to buy into good quality commercial property (i.e. good buildings in good locations with top class tenants bound by long-term leases). Real estate investment trusts have the money required because lots of investors have pooled their funds and own many commercial buildings which gives them a good spread of buildings without being reliant on only a few tenants. Certainly the manager and trustee take a fee but think of the alternative: to invest in commercial property I would be buying older buildings in poorer locations and would be reliant on only a very small number of tenants. By owning property via managed funds, I own 0.001 per cent of something that is really good instead of 100 per cent of something fairly ordinary.

Managed funds do, of course, cost. There are fees to the managers that eat into the returns. This is one of the reasons that I prefer investors to invest directly where they can. However, with difficult markets—offshore markets, high technology, commercial property and so on—I think that you are better to pay a fee and invest in these areas than to not pay a fee and not invest or, perhaps, worst of all to not pay a management fee and invest in an area where you have no competence. If paying a fee lets me access markets that would otherwise be inaccessible, I will pay the fee: the likes of commercial property, China and high tech are too good to turn your back on.

Passive or Active

There are two main types of managed fund. The first type is an actively managed fund. This is a fund where the managers make continuous buy/sell decisions as they try to beat the market. These active managers have an index that they compare their performance to. Whatever the area that they are to invest in will have an index which is essentially an average of performance in that area. For example, if the fund is to invest in healthcare, there will be a healthcare index against which the managers will measure their performance. An active manager tries to pick shares in its sector that will outperform the average as represented by the index. To do this they undertake research and try to employ the best analysts and investor experts. This, of course, costs and the person who ends up paying is the investor.

Passive (or index tracker) funds do not try to beat the average. They simply buy the index and hold it. Their performance is, therefore, average. It should match the index. In fact, it will usually be a little less than the index because even though the costs are lower for a passive fund, there are still some costs and these come off the returns. Passive fund managers simply buy the shares or bonds that are in the index, or sometimes they buy the index itself. This does not require a lot of expertise or time. In fact, a great deal of it is done by computer. This means that such funds are very cheap to run and have very low fees. However, you should recognise that with a passive index tracker, you are never going to get any return over the market average.

So, which is better: actively managed or passive index tracker funds? My answer to this is that on the whole you are better with passive funds. Many active managers do not even perform as well as the index, largely because of the higher costs and fees, and many under-perform. Most fund managers will stick fairly close to the index against which they are measured. They quite deliberately hug the index knowing that they will get heavily criticised by investors if their performance is well below it. Therefore they play for safety and own mostly the shares or bonds that are in the index, only moving outside it a little in an attempt to enhance returns. These index huggers are not usually worth investing in as the upside is very limited while the additional fees mean that there is a considerable downside.

There are, however, managers of active funds who do

not slavishly follow the index. They usually invest in funds that have mandates allowing them to hold cash at times so that when they see a market downturn they sell up a proportion of their shares or bonds and do not follow the index downwards. Even more aggressive are the funds whose mandate allows them to go short. This means that if the fund manager sees a share that they think is overvalued, they are allowed to sell shares in that company even though they do not own those shares. The idea is that when the shares fall to a lower value, the manager can buy the shares cheaper than they had sold for to close out the deal and take the profit. Being able to hold cash and to sell short means that managers' returns (and therefore your returns) can be a long way from the average—on both the upside and the downside. With the ability to hold cash or go short, good managers can give spectacular returns.

The key to managing your investments lies in deciding what kind of investor you are, then deciding where you fit on the investment spectrum. Most investors should get the bulk of their returns in difficult markets by going into passive index tracker funds. You could try to enhance your returns by having a little in actively managed funds or even in a few shares that you think might perform well. No one should ever completely turn their backs on managed funds. I don't think I've ever met an investor who has sufficient diversification without some money in managed funds. Nor, however, should you completely turn your back on direct investment. This may mean having to deal with a share broker but when it comes to investing, there is plenty you can learn to do if you want to.

Chapter

9 Timing

Boom or gloom?

One of the issues with investing for twenty good summers is that most people in this situation get all of their capital in one lump sum through either selling their business or cashing up their superannuation. Having the proceeds from the sale of the business sitting as cash in the bank can be a psychological barrier to investing. Everyone says that you can get much better returns than bank deposits and so you become impatient and keen to get investing. This is where the risk of timing comes into play. Will this prove to be a good time to invest or not?

I have seen many people in this situation who have consulted a financial adviser. The adviser then does their asset allocation and makes specific investment recommend-ations. When the investment plan has been approved, the investments are made—all on the one day. In hindsight, this one day may prove to be the right day or it may prove to be the wrong day. In any event, the day is chosen arbitrarily and if it is a bad day because markets are booming, huge losses happen. This can result in first time investors getting out of the investment markets in disgust.

Remember: *buy in gloom, sell in boom.* It is one of the best pieces of investment advice and perhaps the most frequently ignored. Most people do the exact the opposite of what they are meant to do, buying at the peak of a market and selling into the following trough.

The idea of buying in gloom and selling in boom is not ignored wilfully. There is no conscious effort to go against the advice. In fact, just about everybody would agree that you should buy into markets when everybody else is selling and sell when every body else is buying. Just about everyone would also agree that a counter-cyclical approach is likely to be the most profitable. That the strategy is logical and rational is in no doubt. So why, then, do people not follow it? Why do so many people insist on buying into markets that are booming and selling when the markets are at their most gloomy?

The answer is that people get caught up in the moment. They get swept along by the crowd, buoyed by the noise of the markets as amplified through the media. When markets are booming, the news media is full of the gains that are being made. Regardless of whether it is the property market, bonds or shares, the chatter can get so loud it is almost deafening. More than that, people with vested interests also seize on the opportunity to make more money in buoyant times.

Share brokers and real estate agents ramp up their marketing and other 'experts' suddenly appear promoting their seminars or advisory services. Grandiose claims are often made even when market valuations are way out of line, people will give all sorts of reasons for the extraordinary valuations. You can tell when there is a serious market bubble: the vested interests and some commentators will say, 'this time it is different' and then give some complicated reasons to try to justify the unrealistic asset prices. The end result of all of this is that everyone seems to be making so much money that you decide to join them . . . just as the market peaks.

The reverse is also true: when the markets are gloomy, the noise is also loud and just as difficult to stand up against. It is about when the last optimistic commentator turns into a pessimist that you know that the bottom is not far away. It is into this gloom that most people sell at just about the worst possible time.

Although we all know that we should buy in gloom and sell in boom, most of us do exactly the opposite. Getting caught up in the hype of the markets is one of the biggest causes of investment loss that I know of. In reality, people lose touch with the prime investment fundamental—that they are buying for income. If the income is very low because asset prices have been bid up so far, as happens during booms, you should know that this is a time to sell.

There are a lot of investment experts who say that you cannot time the markets and you should not even try. These experts recognise the trouble that people experience with buying in a boom and selling in gloom and regard trying to time a market as something of a lottery: after you have put your money into an investment, perhaps it will go up or perhaps it will go down. Their argument is to simply make your investment for the very long term and not touch it for years or even decades.

These experts point, in particular, to those who try to trade in and out of an investment as they try to predict its next upwards or downwards move. People who believe you cannot time the markets will show that those who try to predict market movements will have huge losses when they make a comparatively small mistake—that is, they have judged that the market will go down and miss one of the biggest upward days of the decade! These people argue that you should therefore simply invest and stay with the investment for years, ignoring the noise of the markets and the gyrations that will inevitably happen. In this way you will get an average return from the particular investment or asset class.

Can you time the market?

I believe that you can time the market. Even better, I do not think that it is all that difficult to do.

In my opinion, there are clearly times when it is better to buy shares, property or bonds and there are times when you are better to be a selling them. There are good times to be getting into a market and good times to be getting out.

The thing that catches people out is that you cannot judge this timing precisely. There is another investment saying: *Only one person sells at the top or buys at the bottom.* You cannot expect to be able to judge the exact top nor the exact bottom. Only one person gets to be the top seller (or the bottommost buyer) and, given all the players in the market, it is unlikely to be you. However, this does not mean that you cannot distinguish when shares, property or bonds are overvalued or undervalued.

When a market is clearly overvalued, the returns from rents, dividends or interest will reduce. That is a good time to start to sell down what you are holding. You will not get the timing perfect, but at least you will be starting to cash up, reducing your exposure to a market that is getting overheated. Note that I am not saying that you need to sell out completely. In fact, I do not think that you should. It is much more a case of lowering your exposure to the overheated market. In some ways you should see this as taking the profits that you have made from the high-flying market. In any event, if you have set your asset allocation, you will want to rebalance your investments as one of your asset classes has more than its rightful allocation.

Having said all of this, I am a long-term investor. I am not a trader. I would encourage you to be the same. That is, to buy good quality investments and hold them for the long term. I think that you should ignore most of the short-term reactions and noise that come from the market, and only consider selling if and when a major rise turns into a ridiculously over-inflated bubble. This happens periodically, for example the dot com boom of the late 1990s and the property boom of the mid-2000s were clearly bubbles waiting to be burst. No one could get the timing right exactly. No one knew exactly when these bubbles would burst but many of us knew that they would burst one day. We also knew that when they did that there would be great pain.

You will never get your timing into or out of investment markets perfect. No one rings a bell when the market is right at the top or right at the bottom. All that you should be aiming to do is to avoid the worst times to buy or sell and perhaps to try to enhance your returns a little. Most of your returns will come from the overall market. Even the very best investors are unlikely to be able to get returns that are a lot more than the market average.

There are three things that you can do to improve your timing:

1. Do the opposite of what everyone else is doing. This is more an attitude than anything else—it is counter-cyclical and contrarian. However, it is not easy at times to know exactly what 'everybody' else is doing. Nevertheless, when there is a frenzied boom, that is the time to consider selling to rebalance. When there is widespread dismal gloom, that is the time to think about buying.

2. Buy when investments are yielding a good deal of income. High cash yields from interest, rents and dividends reflect the fact that prices are cheap. When experts talk about a particular investment or an overall market being cheap, they are usually referring to the fact that there is high income coming from it.

3. Continually rebalance your portfolio. This is very important for those investing in retirement. It means knowing what your asset allocation should be and sticking to that allocation. When it gets out of line because of the movement in the markets, you should sell the investment that you are now over your allocation in. You should then invest in assets where your percentage invested is lower than benchmark. This effectively means that you will be selling your better performing asset class and buying into the underperforming one (which is selling in boom and buying gloom).

The dangers of a lump sum

The most dangerous time for investors for twenty good summers is right at the start when you are shifting from being a growth investor to an income investor. The lump sum you end up with from selling your business or cashing in your superannuation may be the largest amount of money that you have ever had. What you do with it will dictate the lifestyle that you have for the next 20 or more summers. It is a dangerous time because it is easy to get caught up in the 'exciting' investment of the day (i.e. the market that is currently booming) and get your asset allocation or your timing wrong.

I have seen a lot of clients over the years who have had their lifestyles restrained because of poor market timing. These people had often received their retirement lump sum in the late 1990s and then gone off to a financial adviser or share broker to invest it for income. The international share markets were booming at this time (remember the dot com boom?) and the adviser had set the asset allocation, got the clients approval for it and then invested all of the capital on one day. This often proved to be at the top of the market, or at least very close to the top. A decade later, some of these people were still showing losses, at least on the international equities part of their portfolio. In some cases they continued to show losses across their whole portfolio years later.

Obviously I am eager for people to get financial advice —being an adviser, how could I be anything else? I am especially keen that people get financial advice at this time of life because the transition from wealth building to using capital to get income is such a big change and so important for you to ensure the quality of life that you are going to have. However, the business model that many financial advisers use to get paid—commissions and percentages of funds that have been invested—actively works against good investment.

Because some investment advisers get paid only when investments are made they are incentivised to place all of the available capital into investments as quickly as possible. And that is indeed what tends to happen. Clients are persuaded to invest immediately regardless of the state of the markets. Because of the payment structure used by some financial advisers, they seldom suggest that the investor waits until markets have returned to a normal level.

To be fair, it may be difficult to know exactly what a normal level is and even when we do know, it may be a long wait. Markets can be over-valued, but get even more over-valued. They may stay over-valued for a long time and there can be frustration when you are waiting to invest and therefore missing out on gains. A couple of years holding cash while markets continue to boom can seem like a very long wait! There is a party going on that everybody else has been invited to except you. Similarly, it can seem like a long wait when you buy into markets that are down and they stay down, perhaps for a year or two. This is the trouble with timing the markets. It is difficult unless you are very sure of your valuations and are very patient. It is nearly impossible if you have an adviser who is pressing you to get into the markets.

However, there is a solution. It's called 'dollar cost averaging'.

Dollar cost averaging

Dollar cost averaging works on the premise that it is difficult to time the markets and that it is very risky to try. Much of this book is about reducing risk because when you are investing for your best summers and dependent on your capital for your lifestyle, risk has to be reduced as far as possible. I am usually very happy for younger people to try to time the markets to improve returns because they are less risk averse. Older people are very risk averse and should not try to time the markets to anything like the same extent, if at all. This is why I always use dollar cost averaging for my own investing and for my clients.

Dollar cost averaging takes timing issues out of the equation—it removes timing risk almost completely. Dollar cost averaging is a flash term for drip feeding your capital into the markets gradually over a long period of time. It means making regular small(ish) investments over several years rather than all at one time. This means that some investments are made at good times (i.e. when things are gloomy) while others are made at bad times (i.e. when markets are booming).

Because you make investments at different times, you will get different prices. Over the time period that you are dollar cost averaging into the market, you will get an average price—not spectacularly good, and not spectacularly bad: just average. This may sound somewhat defeatist from someone who usually wants to outperform the markets. However, many people who are investing their life savings simply cannot take the risk of investing all at once when it may prove to be a bad time to invest.

Take a market as represented by the figure below:

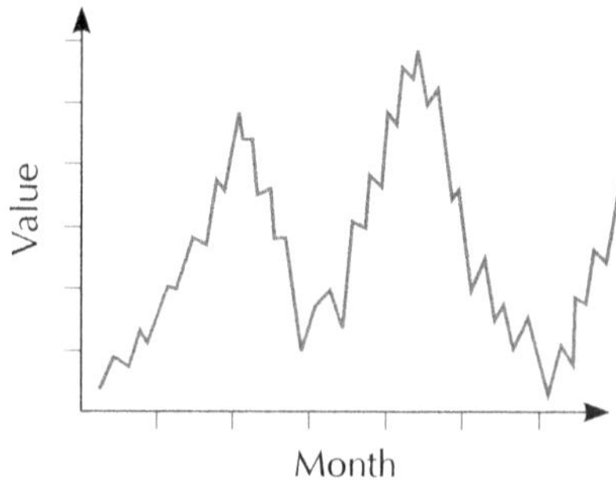

This is clearly a very volatile market—the value of the investments is going up and down a lot. Although it easy to pick the good times and the bad times to buy into the market in hindsight, it is not so easy at the time. If I was to invest in a market like this, I would divide up my money and invest at regular intervals. If this was an investment into shares, I would probably make an investment every quarter over a period of three or four years.

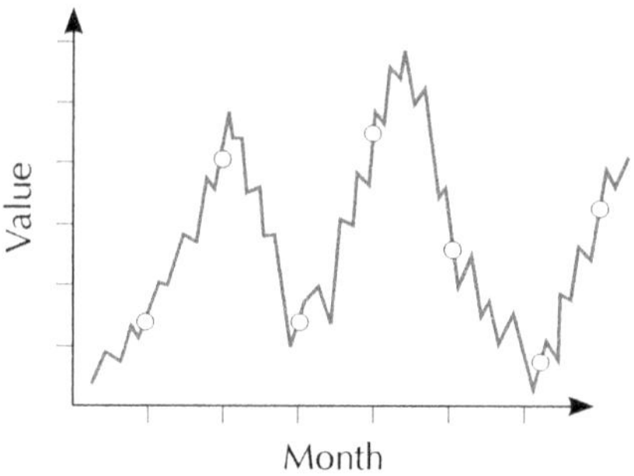

Notice that these investments are made regardless of what the markets are doing—whether they are up or down, booming or gloomy, the investment is still made on the appointed date.

By doing this religiously, you will end up getting an average price over the time period.

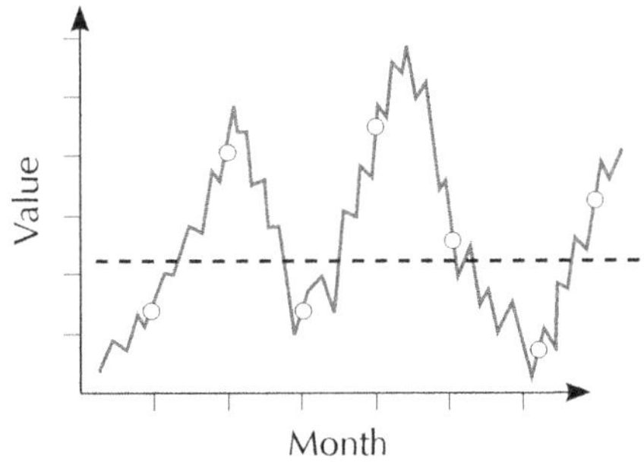

There are some important things to be aware of with dollar cost averaging:

1. You can dollar cost average into any market but you should always use it when going into particularly volatile markets. I use it when buying shares and foreign currency. With some individual shares I might dollar cost average over a quite short time period, perhaps three months. Having identified a good share that represents good value, I would buy into it gradually rather than all at once. However, when building up to a full allocation of shares as set out in your asset allocation plan, I would set a time period of three to five years.

2. Although you may be dollar cost averaging into a particular asset class over several years, you do not have to buy the same particular investment each time. I am somewhat opportunistic in this respect and when it is time to put some more money into a particular asset class, I would look around for

the best opportunity. Those who are taking a more passive approach may go into the same investments each time, which could be two or three index tracking funds, but those who are more active will look around for what seems cheap at the time.

3. You can use dollar cost averaging when you sell. Generally this will be over a shorter period of time than buying in and it is particularly useful when markets are bad. Rather than selling out all on one day, you can sell out in tranches. For example, if you owned 20,000 shares in a company, you might sell 4000 shares each month for five months.

4. You do not have to stick absolutely to the day to make investments. The important thing is that you keep on making investments into the particular market fairly regularly over a long period. For example, I might be due to make another investment into shares in six weeks time, however, if my broker contacted me and said there was a good opportunity to pick up a new listing the next week, I would make that investment.

5. Beware the 'bugger!' factor. If you have an allocation of $120,000 to go into property funds you may dollar cost average this by making a $10,000 investment into funds each quarter for three years. While you are making the first few investments, the property markets boom and you curse that you did not put all of the allocation that you had into the market. That certainly is a downside to dollar cost averaging

but you should console yourself with the knowledge that you have avoided a lot of timing risk and also that you have made good gains from your early investments.

A warning

Most people do not succeed with dollar cost averaging because they do not make their planned investments when times are bad. People make their investments quite happily when markets are booming because they hear the positive noise coming out of the particular market and know good gains are being made. It is when the market goes down that the noise becomes gloomy. This can rattle even quite disciplined investors who will, as a result, not make the planned investment.

This makes no sense: having purchased quite expensive units during the good times, you can only average down the price by continuing to make investments during tough times. If you do not, you are stuck with your expensive units and the losses that you have as the market falls. You must make your planned investments, good times or bad. In fact, being a somewhat contrarian investor, if I was going to shift from my planned dollar cost averaging into a particular market or asset class, I would buy a little less when markets were booming, and a little more when they were down. However, even this can be dangerous so most people would be well advised to stick to the plan.

Dollar cost averaging should not be confused with 'averaging down'. Averaging down is when an investor buys units at, say, $1 only to see the units fall immediately to

80 cents. Such an investor buys more units at 80 cents so that he or she now has an average price of 90 cents. If an investment does fall like this after you have purchased it, buying some more at the lower level might be a good idea. If the investment was a good buy at $1, it is an even better buy at 80 cents. However, it may also be the case that something has happened to the company or trust to cause the price of the units to fall, meaning the price of $1 was not a good buy and it may still not be a good buy at 80 cents A fall like this is an occasion to review what you have bought—if the price of 80 cents is indeed a bargain, then by all means buy more. However, if $1 was a poor purchase and 80 cents is still a poor purchase, you should probably cut your losses and sell out.

Dollar cost averaging is an essential tool for those starting to invest for income in retirement. Go slowly into your new investment strategy, after all, patience is the investor's greatest virtue.

Chapter

10 The place of debt assets

Bonds and deposits

Debt assets—assets when you are lending your money to an enterprise—give stability to a portfolio. Bonds and deposits do not have the volatility that ownership assets have meaning the income from them is more certain. This is not to say that you cannot lose money on bonds and deposits—you can. Bonds can lose value when interest rates rise and even banks have been known to go under. However, the loss of value on bonds is typically much smaller than value loss on shares and, provided the issuer of the bond does not fail, you will continue to receive your interest and, on maturity, the return of your capital. Default among banks is rare and in many countries deposits in banks are guaranteed by the government—and in those countries where there is no government guarantee, there is usually good bank supervision by the central bank.

Debt assets are less risky because if the organisation that has your money fails (be it a bank in the case of a deposits, or a corporate in the case of a bond) you are not last in line to get your money back as an investor is defined as a creditor. When an organisation goes into liquidation, there is a pecking order as to when the various classes of creditors get paid. The people who own the entity are last in this queue—the shareholders or unit holders only get money in liquidation once the creditors have been paid first.

Debt assets also offer a lower level of risk because the investor gets an agreed amount of interest before the owners get any profits. The owners of the enterprise (shareholders or unit holders) have effectively agreed to pay this interest and only after the lenders have been paid their interest do they get what is left over. Sometimes what is left over will be a great deal and sometimes it will be nothing. Providing the company, bank or authority is able, the bond holders or depositors will get paid regardless of what is left as profit.

The quality of bonds and deposits does, of course, vary enormously. The amount of interest that you are paid will (or should) vary with the quality of the issuer. Sometimes, especially when money is easy and there are lots of investors chasing a relatively small number of bonds, the spread between good bonds and deposits and bad ones narrows. In these cases there is not much difference between the interest that is paid for a good investment and a poor one. Another way of looking at this is that the risk of the poor investment is not adequately rewarded by a high enough interest rate and there are certainly times when this happens. In times like this, you should not chase a little extra return for a whole lot more risk. In my view, risk should always be rewarded and when it is not, this should serve as a warning that things are getting out of kilter.

Two things are important for the interest rate that you will be paid for a bond or a deposit:

1. Creditworthiness of the issuer
2. Duration of the investment

Creditworthiness

Creditworthiness is a measure of the likelihood that the entity to which you lend your money will be able to pay interest and also repay your capital on maturity. Creditworthiness is also a measure of whether the borrower is likely to default on their obligations.

There is, of course, a wide spectrum on creditworthiness—on the one hand we have stable, democratic governments borrowing money, and on the other hand small finance companies directed by people with dodgy pasts and probably even more dodgy futures. Governments are considered to have the best credit risks. This is because they have the ability to tax their populations and they don't have to wait for customers to give them money: if they are hard up they simply increase taxes. In spite of this, governments have been known to be unable to meet their obligations—there is no such thing as a risk free investment. Some governments who are struggling to meet their obligations have also managed to inflate their way out of trouble. By this I mean that a government that is loaded up with a great deal of debt is helped by inflation because the repayment of their debts is made with money that is worth a good deal less than when it was when borrowed. Governments can create inflation which, although not usually desirable, can be a good thing for them if they have too much debt.

Obviously, then, there are governments and there are governments—not all are created equal: the government of Chad is unlikely to be as creditworthy as the government of Switzerland. This is the same with other borrowers who issue bonds and who take deposits: local authorities (which are also regarded as very safe because they also can tax via rates), banks (safe because they are usually supervised by a central bank or have their deposits guaranteed by governments), corporates and others. Ultimately creditworthiness comes down to the credit risk of the particular entities that you are lending to.

You are unlikely to have the skills to properly measure credit risk and, even if you did, it would be a huge job to do this on all of the issuers and deposit takers that you might want to invest with. Moreover, if you fronted up to the headquarters of Microsoft and said that you were assessing them because you were thinking of buying $30,000 of their bonds, you probably would not get much of a reception.

The job of assessing credit risk belongs with the rating agencies, of whom Moody's, Fitch, and Standard and Poor's are the most well known, although there are plenty of others. Generally these firms are not hired by investors. Instead it is the borrowers who call the rating agency and ask to be assessed, and then pay the bill for the service.

A bond issuer or a bank taking deposits knows that it needs to have its credit risk assessed or investors will not buy its bonds or deposit funds with it. The borrower gets in one or more of the rating agencies and opens it books to let them have a look at what is going on. Obviously, the borrower will tell the agency how wonderful everything is and it is the agency's job to find the negative things.

The borrower gives the rating agency information that would not be generally available to the public. The agency then carries out a detailed financial analysis of the borrower, looking at all aspects of the operation—its assets, liabilities, income, expenses, commitments, customers and so on. They also look at the ownership structure, governance matters, management capability and risk issues. By the time the rating agency has finished and written a rating, there will not be too much that they do not know about the enterprise.

The better the rating that the borrower can get, the less interest they will have to pay. This probably results in a bit of tension between the agency and the borrower. The rating is usually a series of letters, from AAA down to D, with plus or minus signs to denote gradations. Generally, anything above BBB is regarded as 'investment grade'. Unfortunately, the series of letters is not standardised across the various rating agencies. I often wish that they would all simply use a standard scale of one to 50.

The investment rating that is given is obviously relative to other borrowers. There is no absolute guarantee. The grade is really about the likelihood that the borrower will default over a certain time period, so for a certain grade, you might expect the borrower to default once every fifty years. This is not to say that credit rating agencies always get things right. There will be things that they miss regardless of how good their systems and processes are. In any event, remember that they are only measuring risk, not absolutes.

Clearly, the better the rating, the lower the interest rate that you as an investor will get. Investment theory says that there should be a nice neat line describing the risk and return equation. Although there will be a very clear correlation between the interest rate paid and the creditworthiness as measured by rating agencies, at any point in time it will not be perfect. There will always be some investments where risk is not being properly rewarded or where investors are getting a better return than they should given the rating.

This is particularly so on the secondary market (see page 142). A bond with a ten-year maturity may get traded many times during its life. The financial position of the entity that issued the bond (government, bank or other corporate) will change and the market will continually try to guess how the issuer is performing.

The ratings agency will continue to update the issuer's rating over time. This may be on a regular basis, but if something major happens (for example, a government starts to run budget deficits, or a corporate successfully starts to sell a new profitable product) the agency may put the issuer on credit watch. This credit watch may be positive or negative and is usually only held for a short time until the rating agency has had a chance to have a look at the entity in detail. However, at all times, participants in the debt markets will be making their own assessments of borrowers and buying and selling accordingly.

As an adviser, I almost always recommend to clients that they take low-risk debt investments. This part of the portfolio is to give stability and to reduce volatility. While you want to get good returns from all parts of your investment portfolio, it does not seem sensible to me to take great risks with bonds or deposits by investing in entities that are low on the creditworthiness scale. Let your shares and property provide enhanced returns as they will also give you some volatility and that should be quite enough given that you have a low appetite for risk. This is why I recommend that clients use main street banks for their deposits and government stock and good corporates for their bonds. There are plenty of fringe investments in both areas—beware of chasing high returns with these.

Duration of investments

The duration of an investment will dictate how much interest is paid. You would expect that the interest for a five-year bond would be different from a 30-day deposit, even if the issuer is the same (or at least has the same credit-worthiness). For example, a bank might offer a range of term deposits, from 30 days through to five years. If you look at the interest rates that are on offer for each of these you might find that for 30 days you are getting a rate of 6 per cent and for five years a rate of 7.5 per cent. This is called the yield curve.

Usually, the longer the duration of an investment, the greater the amount of interest that will be paid. When the market is like this it is said that to have a 'positive yield curve'. This is a normal state of affairs—you would usually expect that the longer your money is tied up for, the greater the risk and therefore the more interest paid. An extreme example of this would be 30-year bonds (which are quite common in some countries). To lock your money up with a fixed rate of interest for 30 years is a big call—anything can happen in that time. There might be inflation running at 10 per cent—which would make the 4.75 per cent that you are getting on your 30-year bond look very unattractive. This remains the case even though there is a secondary market for these bonds, allowing the investor to sell out at any time within the 30-year period. However, if inflation did kick in at 10 per cent during the period of the bond, interest rates would have risen and the buyer of your bond would pay a much lower price than you originally paid for it so that he or she could get the interest rate prevailing at the time.

There are a lot of possible things that could happen over the years, many of them adverse, so investors usually demand more interest for longer maturity bonds.

There are times when there is a negative yield curve, when longer maturity debts attract less interest than short-term deposits. This usually reflects the market's belief that interest rates are likely to fall across the yield curve and they have therefore moved to lock in an interest rate for a longer term.

As an investor looking for income, you would want a spread of maturities across your portfolio. You do want some cash or, at least, short-term deposits. You also want to lock in rates for several years with longer-dated fixed-interest bonds. However, you do not want all of your bonds maturing at once as this may prove to be a time when interest rates are down. Many investors try to establish their portfolios so that each year they have a part of their bond portfolio maturing. This means that they have a spread of maturities averaging out interest rates over a long period of time.

Cash and short-term deposits

I usually think of cash and short-term deposits as having a maturity of less than a year, although most of them will be shorter in duration. Mostly, they will be bank deposits such as savings accounts and term deposits. I recommend that these be liquid investments, which are able to be cashed up at any time. The main benefit of these investments is, in fact, that they are liquid. The main purpose of liquidity is described in chapter 7—it is for you to have a reservoir of cash and short-term deposits to tide you over when other parts of the portfolio are not performing. This is a critical part of your investment management if you are to avoid becoming a forced seller.

The other purpose of cash and short-term deposits is as a store of wealth when times are buoyant so that you are able to take advantage of opportunities when the markets turn downwards. In this respect, holding a high proportion of cash can be seen as a very aggressive stance. There are times—they come along about once a decade—where markets get far too high. If you had a market neutral view, you would continue to own your planned allocation in that market, selling down only to keep the right allocation. This is a fairly passive stance but what many advisers would say is the right thing to do. However, if you took the strong view that the markets had gone to a level which was unsustainably high, you might sell everything to hold cash while you wait for the market to correct. This is an aggressive stance as the correction may not come for years.

My view is that there are times when markets get far too high and you do not want to be a part of them—think of the craziness of the dot com boom in the late 1990s or the global housing boom of the 2000s. Both of these markets got far too high and were unsupported by the amount of income that could come off the investments. I took no part in either—the income was just not there and I regard myself as a fundamentalist investor. Sure, I missed out on profits as the speculative bubble continued and continued. However, I slept at night and if I had been in those markets at the time, I would not have slept as the paltry amount of income did not sustain the values that the markets were driven up to.

There is an opportunity cost to holding cash but usually that is the only cost. There is an old market saying: *If in doubt, stay out.* In other words, if a market or an investment is looking overvalued, hold cash. I am always happy for my clients to hold cash while they are waiting for a better opportunity. It is true that over long periods of time you can do better but as a low-risk investor, you do not want to be killed in the short term. Patience is a great virtue in investing so you should be prepared to wait out a boom as you can be sure that if there is little prospect of high income from the investment that it will correct and eventually come back to a more realistic level.

It may seem like a long wait but you should know that there are always good opportunities coming. You do not need to let your money burn a hole in your pocket and find yourself stampeded into buying something that is overvalued. While you are waiting, your cash will be safe in the bank earning interest, (perhaps in a couple of different banks if you want to spread risk further) and ready for when you need it.

Bonds

Bonds give stability to a portfolio. This is not because their value remains constant—their value moves around as interest rates rise and fall and the creditworthiness of the issuer changes. Instead, stability is given to the portfolio by bonds because the income from them is fixed and known for long periods of time. This is different from cash and short-term deposits, which mature quite soon with their interest rates set regularly, meaning that you are at risk of the rate dropping. Moreover, the yield curve is usually positive, meaning that your cash and short-term deposits will have a lower interest rate. Therefore, anyone investing for income needs to have a good amount of bonds in the portfolio.

Bonds are issued by all sorts of organisations and entities to raise funds. When a new bond is issued, the issuer will set an interest rate at a level that will attract the market without it costing the issuer any more than necessary. To set this interest rate, the issuer and its advisers will look at the state of the markets, the price of bonds from organisations with a similar credit rating and the duration of the bonds to be issued. This interest rate that is set is called the coupon rate.

When the bonds are issued, as far as the issuer is concerned, that is the end of the matter—they simply have to pay the interest each period and repay the capital on maturity. From the issuer's point of view, they will hope that there is a lot of inflation so that they can make their payments with deflated dollars. However, from the investor's point of view, bond issue is not necessarily the end of the matter. Most bonds have a secondary market. That is, investors can, if they want, sell their bonds on a market which is not dissimilar to the share market. A bond may have been issued initially at $1 to give a certain coupon rate. However, with movements in the interest rate markets, the bond may later sell for more or less than $1 to reflect a yield to the new purchasing bond owner that reflects the prevailing rate. The bond issuer will continue to pay the same coupon rate, however the new investor will receive a different yield from the bond depending on what he or she has paid for it.

Bond markets can be very busy, with a lot of players

buying and selling. Investors may want to sell their bonds for one of two reasons:

1. They need some cash. I would hope that this is not the case as it would represent a major mistake in money management. Bond maturities should be set for a time when you are going to need your money back. Bond markets can be volatile. Their values go up and down all the time. As with shares, you do not want to be in a forced-seller situation—you may be selling at a time when interest rates have risen and your bonds are therefore worth less. You should hold a bond portfolio with maturities that are spread out over a period of time and you should arrange your money so that you can hold your bonds through to maturity.

2. Bond traders may want to cash up to take profits that they have made on their bonds, or to avoid a loss that seems imminent. There are a lot of traders in bond markets, mostly, but not entirely, professional fund managers, who regularly trade bonds. These people are watching what is happening in the interest rate market and keep a fixed eye on the issuers whose bonds they have. I do not recommend that private investors try to become traders in bonds, however there are times when you might want to sell out of certain bonds because you can foresee changes coming up to the market that will be beneficial or adverse to the value of your bonds. For private investors this will be rare, nevertheless there will be times when you will want to sell out.

Bonds are an important part of any income investor's portfolio. It is also an area that will probably grow in importance as you get older. Many people slowly reduce the property and share part of the portfolio as they get older, increasing the bonds that they have. As you get older and the number of good summers decreases, you do not need the growth so much and you can lower risk further by selling shares and property and buying bonds. For some this may be a depressing thought: getting old is no fun. The important thing is to have a lot of fun while you get there.

Chapter 11 The place of ownership assets

Shares and property

Ownership assets are distinguished by the fact that you are the owner of the underlying business or property. This means a number of things:

1. You get the profits when all expenses have been paid—these profits may be very big or they may be very small (or even non-existent depending on how well the enterprise performs). Debt investors are limited to taking an agreed interest rate but there is no such limit on the owners of a business or property. There are blue-sky possibilities but also the possibility of the doss house.

2. In the event of failure and liquidation, creditors, including the debt investors, will get their money back first. The owners only get paid if there is something left over after the assets have been sold and creditors repaid.

3. The value of shares and profits will go up and down a great deal more than debt investments will. Ownership assets have greater volatility risk. Those who have ownership should therefore expect higher returns because they are taking greater risks.

People investing for twenty good summers are risk averse. However, there are a number of risks that they face and one of those is inflation. You are likely to be investing over a long period of time—certainly a couple of decades and potentially a lot longer. Therefore you need some investments that will give greater returns. If you solely invest in debt assets, your income will not grow but your cost of living will. If you invest only in debt assets as a 60-year-old and got an interest return of $25,000 pa, twenty years later you will still be getting $25,000 pa, assuming there has been no major structural change in interest rates. However, if you want to maintain your standard of living as an eighty year old you will be disappointed. Assuming an inflation rate of 2.5 per cent, you will need income of over $40,000 pa to enjoy the same standard of living. Perhaps you could argue that at 80 you do not need as much income as you do at 60. There is some truth in this—on average our expenditures fall as we get older. However, you cannot be sure that you will be happy with only 60 per cent of the spending power that you once had.

The place of ownership assets is, then, to give you higher returns so that you keep your spending power up and continue to do the things that you have planned. Shares and property give two returns:

1. Income from dividends and rent. In some cases, these can be quite high, at times even being close to the cash returns received from debt investments.

2. Capital growth. Both shares and property appreciate over time, sometimes the capital growth component being the larger part of your total returns.

However, there is something else that ownership investments give: income growth.

Income growth

The growth in your income they provide over time is one of the most important reasons for you to have shares and property in your portfolio. Debt investments pay a return that is fixed for a period of time. Generally, when a debt investment matures, you do not get a higher rate of interest under renewal. If you do get a higher rate it is because at the time there will have been higher inflation and that will have eroded the earning power of your capital, so you will be worse off. There are plenty of examples from the past where people have allowed their capital, and therefore their incomes, to erode with inflation.

The key thing is that with ownership assets not only does your capital grow, but over long periods of time, the income grows in line with that capital growth. This is very important and is one of the reasons (in fact, the main reason) that I would usually have an income investor with a relatively large part of the portfolio in ownership assets. Of course, the medium- and long-term growth in income does not go in a nice, straight, predictable line—we should be so lucky!

At times, income will rise sharply while at other times it will remain static or even fall. You also have to recognise that sometimes income from ownership assets will actually stop, perhaps through loss of a tenant or a major business problem. When this happens, you get hit by a double whammy because the value of your investments falls with the decline in income. Although I favour a fairly heavy weighting towards ownership assets, this is why I am very careful about the type of shares or property that I would recommend and why I am very much in favour of a cash buffer (see chapter 7).

Income growth means that eventually you will receive more income from an ownership asset than you will from debt assets. While you may only get an initial dividend yield of 6 per cent on some shares that you buy and you could have got 8 per cent from a bond, in time when you compare your dividends and rents to your purchase price, you will be getting more in dividends and rents. The value of the shares or property will move up so a new buyer will not get the same percentage yield that you get. Those who have been investors for longer will be getting a very good return on their initial purchase price.

Shares

The place of shares is to enhance returns—to give good income, capital appreciation and, perhaps most importantly, income growth. Shares probably give the best investment over long periods of time—better than property, bonds and deposits. However, as you would expect, they are also the most risky asset class as shares are very volatile. This means that many income investors do not own shares. They are rightly frightened of the volatility and can wrongly be frightened of the jargon and market noise that surrounds share investing.

Both of these fears can be alleviated to some extent by owning shares via managed funds. The fear of volatility should be alleviated by investing via managed funds because most funds give greater diversification, which reduces volatility. Owning shares via managed funds also alleviates the fear that comes from the noise of the markets because if you can identify a good managed fund that is based on the market or kind of shares that you want to own, you can almost set and forget. If you have a lot of trust in the fund manager, you can be a bit more relaxed when the market is going down and there is a lot of noise in the news media about what is likely to happen.

In this respect, I prefer managed funds where the mandate allows the manager to hold cash and even to sell shares short. There are many share market managed funds where the manager must be 100 per cent invested in shares at all times. This means that even though it is obvious that a more defensive position is warranted, the managers have to keep invested in the market that the fund is based on. However, some funds allow the manager to sell shares and hold cash allowing the market to go down. Some funds also allow the manager to sell short, selling shares that they do not own and buying them back when they have fallen in value and so profiting from the price difference.

I personally invest in direct shares as well as managed funds that are based on shares. Therefore, I get some of my exposure to the overall markets via managed funds, but also own some individual companies which I think will perform well. I enjoy identifying, researching and purchasing companies and find that many people who are retired are the same—shares can be a fascinating (if somewhat frustrating) 'hobby'. In particular, I have managed funds for the offshore markets as I know less about these.

Perhaps the best way of managing volatility is to buy

shares that produce income in good times and in bad. These tend to be shares in things like water companies, electricity suppliers and toll companies. While many of these companies do not show great growth, they are steady performers and tend to be less affected by downturns. The consistent income that they produce means that they will continue to be good investments even when many other companies are failing to make good profits.

Nevertheless, there will always be volatility in shares and you can never completely shield yourself from it. This part of your portfolio will at times show losses, you simply have to expect that. The important thing is that you are sufficiently diversified across your portfolio so that the total portfolio does not go into a loss situation. This is why I would seldom recommend that an income investor who is reliant on investment returns to fund their lifestyle would hold as much as 40 per cent in shares in their portfolio. Even at that, I would recommend that these shares be largely defensive income shares and very well diversified around the world and across varying industries.

The return from shares can come from both capital growth and income growth or a combination of both. Most people investing for income are primarily concerned with the dividend part of this equation. They look for shares that are likely to pay high dividends. Generally, these are utility companies, infrastructure and mature industrials. These kinds of things do have several advantages for income investors:

- They pay out high dividends. Many of these companies are not looking to expand greatly and can therefore pay out a large percentage of their profits to shareholders by way of dividends.

- They tend to be fairly low risk. The kinds of things that they do—road tolls, electricity generation, water reticulation, food manufacture—are fairly recession-proof because people have to use their products and services regardless. Someone once told me that toilet paper was the most recession proof product—there is little discretion whether to use it or not.
- Their relatively high income also makes them low risk. If the shares in these kinds of things fall, the dividend yield rises, making them very attractive.
- They have a track record and a proven business model in areas where there is unlikely to be much change. This contrasts with companies like Google, whose technology and business model can easily be leapfrogged by someone else, just as Google leapfrogged others a decade or so ago.

At times, shares in infrastructure and utility companies can show dividend yields that are not far from those of bonds. However, they do not often have great capital growth. There is usually a trade-off between capital gain and dividend yield. The companies that usually have stellar capital growth are usually very low dividend yielding, do not have a long and illustrious record of profitable trading and are therefore likely to be most volatile.

Be an investor

Note that this book is about investing not trading. There are plenty of people who have retired and spend their days at their computers trading shares. Some people I know spend their evenings or very early mornings also trading shares because they operate in overseas markets. Other people regard their share trading as their core business—it is what they do and it is how they define themselves. They are buying shares and holding them for a few days or weeks before selling out and banking the profits or wincing at the losses. They regard those profits as their income in the same way that a retailer regards their profits as a way of buying groceries.

I know that some of these people are successful, but not very many of them. In my experience, traders are much happier to tell you about their successes but keep fairly quiet about what has not gone so well.

Whatever the overall success rate for traders, I would always limit any trading to a fairly small amount of money. There are occasionally small opportunities to take a quick profit for people who watch the equity markets closely. Mostly this is stagging—the process of buying into an initial public offering (IPO) before the company lists and selling out immediately on listing. Other opportunities require more judgment and are more risky. Much of this trading is a good deal easier in hindsight.

Actually picking short-term movements before they happen is possible but does not occur as often as some people will have you believe. In any event, you should not allow the occasional opportunistic trade to detract you from your core activity—investing. Buying a share in a business that has good and growing income so that you get dividends and capital growth is likely to be far more profitable and reliable for you than trying you hand at short-term trades. Trading, and this includes stagging, should only be thought of as an occasional bonus.

Shares vary a great deal in their place in any portfolio. Some give only capital growth with very low or no dividends whereas others pay quite high dividends. Given that you are looking for income from your investment capital to fund your lifestyle, you will mostly look for high dividend shares. However, I would say again that you should not ignore low-dividend, high-growth shares—you can always sell a few shares to fund your lifestyle.

One of the good aspects of shares is that they are liquid. While I do believe that liquidity is overpriced and that liquid investments tend to be far more expensive than they should be, being able to sell at any time is a positive attribute of shares. Liquidity is, however, a double-edged sword.

The ease with which you can sell shares means that you may well be influenced by the noise that constantly surrounds the markets. You are likely to be a long-term investor, while much of the noise from commentators is about short-term prospects. It may be true that the market is heading for a fall, although usually by the time the commentators are shouting about the fall it has already happened. In most circumstances you are better to hold onto the shares that you have in good companies through good times and bad.

Property

Property, like shares, gives capital and income growth. It also gives quite good yield—usually better than the yield from many shares. Income growth should at least match inflation making property an ideal asset for those wanting income from their investment capital.

As an investor, I have a great preference for commercial property rather than residential property. In fact, commercial property makes a great investment for income investors and I often recommend that clients have as much as 20 per cent of it in their portfolios, almost always via managed funds called real estate investment trusts (REITs).

The problems with residential property include:

- It is low yielding.
- It is subject to political interference (for example, through rent freezes or tax changes).
- The residential market is often driven by sentiment rather than the income that comes from it.
- Residential tenants can constitute the worst nightmare imaginable, especially when the Hells Angels move in next door.
- It requires a great deal of time to manage, so much so that there are very few managed funds based on residential property. When time to manage is costed in properly, residential property is often not a great deal.
- You are already likely to own a significant amount of residential property—the one that you live in.

Of all these things, it is the yield that is most important. It is yield that you need to fund your lifestyle and commercial property gives much better yield than residential property. Even better than that, the yield that comes from good REITs is steady, predictable and likely to grow in line with inflation. It is hard to see a much better deal than that!

Quite frequently I see clients who are about to start to ease back or retire and who already own a portfolio of residential property. Quite often, it is this property portfolio that has grown their wealth and, because it is well geared, the client has made a lot of money out of it. This is not a good portfolio to take into retirement. The geared residential property is good for growing wealth but it is not a good income-generating asset. It can often be quite the opposite, it is making cash losses which, while they have been useful for tax purposes, are not good for what investors now need, which is to purchase groceries. My advice is to start to sell down the geared property portfolio, using the proceeds of the sale first to pay off debt and, second, to invest in other areas to give diversification. Some people are quite resistant to selling their investment properties. They have spent years building the portfolio, it has done well for them and they are quite proud of it.

There are few people who would want to go into retirement with more than one residential property in their portfolios. Assuming that you were to have 20 per cent of your portfolio in property and your residential property was valued at $400,000, you would need to have a portfolio of $2 million if your asset allocation was to be in line with the benchmark. Moreover, the residential property that you owned would be low yielding and require management that might cramp your lifestyle. Perhaps worst of all, there is no diversification within the property part of your portfolio. The case against residential property for the property allocation of your portfolio is really quite strong and the case for using commercial property REITs is quite compelling.

In praise of REITs

Commercial property is higher yielding with lower management and maintenance than residential property. However, few of us can afford to buy commercial property and even when we can, we can only afford to buy one or two. Just like residential property, this would mean a lack of diversification within the property allocation. Worse, in the case of commercial property, it is likely to mean a very high reliance on a very small number of commercial tenants. Assuming you do not have the wealth to buy high-rise buildings with multiple tenants, you will be very exposed to the financial success of just one or two tenants for your cash flow. Nearly all of the difficulties that are inherent to investing in commercial property can be alleviated by owning the property part of your portfolio via REITs.

REITs have a very simple business model: they raise money from the investing public and use the funds to buy commercial property. They usually add to the amount of money raised from the public by borrowing and are typically geared to about 30 per cent. There are REITs based on all types of commercial property—retail, industrial, office—and also geographically spread around the world. REITs are listed on a share market allowing investors to very easily and cheaply sell out. Because REITs have so much money in property, usually billions of dollars, they own many properties with hundreds or thousands of tenants. The quality of the property that REITs own is usually top class—well-located, good buildings with many very high-class tenants like large corporates and governments.

The advantages of REITs for an income investor are:

- They are quite high yielding. The yield will change over time as the market for property goes up and down and rentals fluctuate. However over time you should get a good yield, certainly one that is higher than you'd get from residential property.
- They allow you to diversify across property types—retail, industrial and office—and also into markets around the world.
- They own top-class properties with the best tenants. I would always rather own a small part of something that is really good rather than 100 per cent of something that is fairly ordinary.
- They allow you to easily and cheaply sell down a part of your holding if you need to convert some of your capital gains into cash. This effectively turns what is usually an illiquid asset class into a liquid one.

The main downside of REITs is that you have to pay someone to manage the trust for you. The fees that the managers charge eat into your returns. However, as an investor I am happy to pay this as it allows me to invest in a very good asset class in a way that is very easy and efficient. REITs give the best access to commercial property for all but the very wealthiest investor.

Shares and property do have a place in the portfolios of income investors. To me a portfolio based solely on bonds and bank deposits makes little sense for most people. It may be that you love share investing, in which case you are about to have a lot more time to devote to your hobby. If you do not love shares, use managed funds for the share part of the portfolio along with the property part. However, do not just ignore them—they are too big a part of the investment universe for that.

Afterword

I have often thought that investment is a great game. It involves thinking about the future, picking the big trends and then working out how to play those trends for investment profit. Watching how things pan out can be fascinating—not everything goes as you would expect, but when it does it is immensely satisfying. The game of investment can be an absorbing pursuit.

However, to call investment a 'game' is to almost certainly downgrade its importance. Investment is not a game in the sense that rugby or basketball are games. These are things that can be played hard, but no-one who loses really suffers. The 'game' of investment, however has big stakes—lose and your life is affected adversely. The points that you score in the investment 'game' enhance your lifestyle—the penalty points that you have deducted can result in reduced means to the point of penury. Investment game? No, it is a serious business with the quality of your most important summers at stake.

With this in mind there are three important pieces of advice which need to be underlined:

1. Plan your change in investment strategy early. This is a major change and needs a great deal of thought.
2. Take advice. This is not a time to skimp to try to save some money. Find an adviser you trust and if he or she does not work out, find another one.

3. Take your time. The transition should not be hurried—easing back from work and adopting an investment strategy that will give income from your capital can be a major dislocation.

Starting to live on the capital that you have accumulated is scary—it is unlikely to be something that you have done before. Nor is it something that you can practice—from the time that you place your very first investment you are putting your portfolio and therefore your lifestyle at risk.

It is time to do the things that you have always wanted to do—if you do not live the life of your dreams now, you are never going to. Live like you are going to die tomorrow, invest like you are going to live forever.

Printed in Dunstable, United Kingdom

91218891R00092